Findings from the 2014 Labor Force Survey
in Sierra Leone

A WORLD BANK STUDY

Findings from the 2014 Labor Force Survey in Sierra Leone

David Margolis, Nina Rosas, Abubakarr Turay, and Samuel Turay

WORLD BANK GROUP

ISBN (paper): 978-1-4648-0742-8
ISBN (electronic): 978-1-4648-0754-1
10.1596/978-1-4648-0742-8

Cover photo: Samantha Zaldivar

Cover design: Debra Naylor, Naylor Design, Inc.

Library of Congress Cataloging-in-Publication Data has been requested

Contents

Findings from the 2014 Labor Force Survey in Sierra Leone
http://dx.doi.org/10.1596/978-1-4648-0742-8

Figures

Maps

Tables

Acknowledgments

This report has been prepared by a team comprising Abubakarr Turay and Samuel Turay (Statistics Sierra Leone) and David N. Margolis (Paris School of Economics, Centre National de la Recherche Scientifique), Nina Rosas, and Rosa Vidarte (World Bank). It was prepared as part of a broader technical assistance initiative of the World Bank to the government of Sierra Leone for the 2014 Labor Force Survey, which has been conducted in close collaboration with the Deutsche Gesellschaft für Internationale Zusammenarbeit and the International Labour Organization (ILO). The technical assistance has been financed by the Korea Trust Fund for Economic and Peacebuilding Transitions. Excellent field support for the survey has been provided by Abu Kargbo (Social Protection Operations Officer), Samantha Zaldivar Chimal (Social Protection Consultant), Andrea Martin (Monitoring and Evaluation Consultant), Hector Zamora (Field Coordinator), and Adam Hoar (Field Coordinator).

Invaluable inputs in the survey design, implementation, and analysis process have been provided by other colleagues in the World Bank, including Kathleen Beegle (Program Leader), Markus Goldstein (Lead Economist), Talip Kilic (Senior Economist, Surveys), Kristen Himelein (Senior Poverty Economist), Suleiman Namara (Senior Social Protection Economist), Hardwick Tchale (Senior Agricultural Economist), Kebede Feda (Economist), Kaliope Azzi-Huck (Education Operations Officer), Frances Gadzekpo (Senior International Finance Corporation Operations Officer), Susan Kayonde (Trade and Competitiveness Consultant), Mauro Testaverde (Economist), and Ning Fu (Social Protection Consultant), as well as by Yacouba Diallo (Senior Statistician, ILO). Insightful peer review comments have also been provided by Thomas Bossuroy (Economist) and Vasco Molini (Senior Economist). The photos were taken by Andrea Martin, Samantha Zaldivar, and Hector Zamora.

Executive Summary

Background

This report seeks to contribute to solutions to the jobs challenge in Sierra Leone through a foundational analysis of the country's first specialized labor survey in nearly three decades. Jobs are critical to poverty reduction and inclusive growth in Sierra Leone, where more than half the population is poor and most are dependent on labor earnings. Adding to the jobs challenge is the young and growing population and therefore the need for substantial job creation, coupled with low labor intensity in the mining sector, which has been driving recent growth. Beyond job creation, in a context where most workers are engaged in low-productivity jobs, improving the quality of jobs is critical for poverty reduction. Given that Sierra Leone is a postconflict country, jobs are also central to sustained stability. Yet, despite the importance of jobs for Sierra Leone, the design of policies and interventions to promote these opportunities has been constrained by a limited knowledge base. This report seeks to narrow these gaps by providing a picture of the jobs landscape based on the country's first labor force survey since 1984.

Overview of Sierra Leone's Labor Market

Most of the country's working-age population is in the labor force, and women participate almost as much as men (figure ES.1). Over 65 percent of Sierra Leone's working-age population, which represents nearly 2 million people, participates in the labor market. Of those people working, the differences between men and women are small (65.7 percent participation among men; 64.7 percent participation among women). Young women are much more likely than young men to be in the labor market (39.4 percent vs. 29.5 percent, using the definition of the International Labour Organization [ILO]), although this gap fades with age.

Among those who do not participate in the labor market, the main reason is attendance at school or training programs. Overall, 54.1 percent of the inactive population was in school or in training. The second most frequent explanation

Figure ES.1   Sierra Leone's Key Labor Market Indicators, by Gender

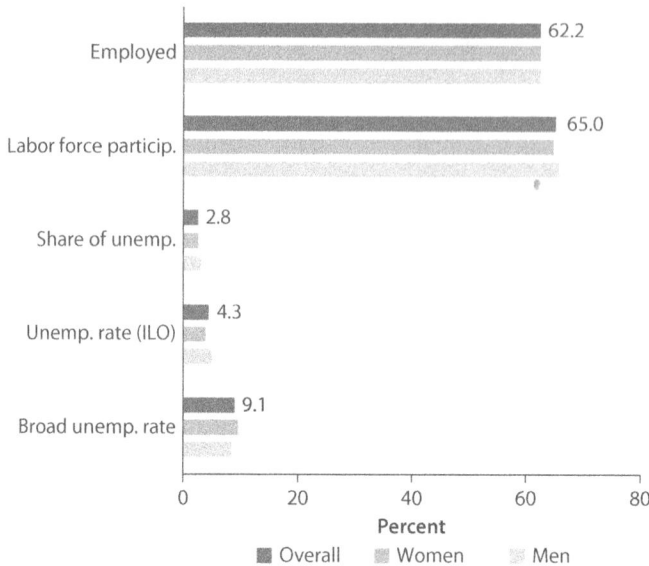

(16.1 percent) for not participating in the labor market is lack of financial or other resources for starting a new business. Taking care of their own household or family affects 9.8 percent of the nonparticipants, and the lack of skill requirements or experience was cited by 4.5 percent as their reason for not participating. Much more than men, women report that family responsibilities are the reason they do not participate.

Unemployment is relatively low, but this masks significant variation across districts and subgroups. Of the working-age population, 62.2 percent were employed, and 2.8 percent were unemployed, as defined by the ILO.[1] The most significant variation in employment rates was across age groups, education levels, urban–rural status, and regions. The highest employment rates were found in rural areas and among the most (and least) well educated. Unemployment rates varied substantially across population subgroups. The highest rates were found among youth, men, migrants, urban residents, especially in the Western Area, and among those with at least an upper-secondary education.

Most workers are employed in relatively low-productivity jobs in farm and nonfarm self-employment; fewer than 10 percent are in wage employment.[2] The vast majority (59.2 percent) of employed individuals aged 15–64 work in agricultural self-employment (see map ES.1). Another 31.3 percent work in nonagricultural self-employment, mostly in microenterprises as traders or shopkeepers. Unpaid workers add an additional 7 percent to total employment. After agriculture (61 percent of all jobs), the service sector is the second-largest employer at a national scale (33 percent),

Map ES.1 Types of Jobs, by District

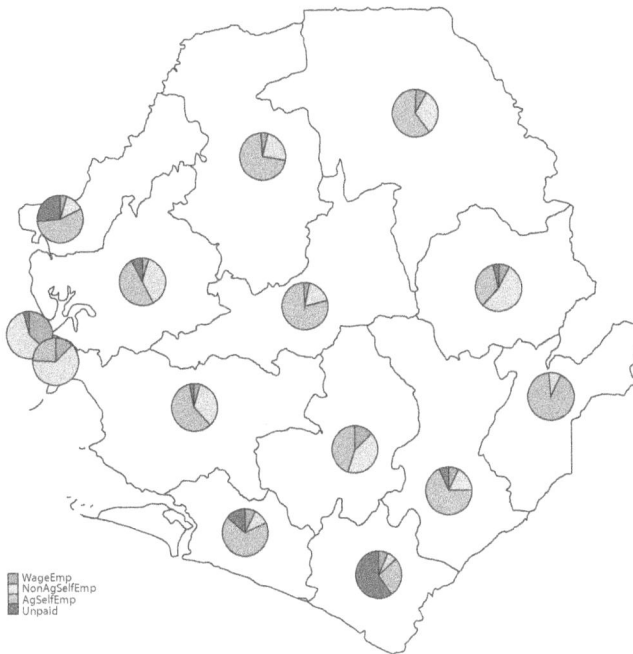

although there is significant regional variation. Personal networks are important for the labor market as the majority of the workforce—especially those with lower educational attainment—seek and obtain their jobs through family and friends.

Capital is a key constraint to entry into the labor force. Over two-thirds of the 9 percent who are broadly unemployed were not actively seeking work.[3] Over half (56 percent) of the broadly unemployed who were not searching for work lacked the capital or resources to start a business; ongoing schooling was the second most frequent explanation (11 percent). Lack of skills was cited by 10 percent, while only 8 percent were discouraged or thought no jobs were available, and less than 1 percent did not want to work. The lack of search effort varies across regions and subgroups. Fewer broadly unemployed women actively search relative to their male counterparts (25 percent vs. 38 percent). The highly educated tend to search more (70 percent) than those with no education (20 percent).

A significant proportion of employed workers would like to work more hours, and the share is higher in Freetown and among certain subgroups. Almost one-third of all workers would like to work more hours. The share is 47 percent in Freetown, compared with 32 percent in rural areas. Nearly one-third of part-time workers are working less than they would like. Underemployment is

Findings from the 2014 Labor Force Survey in Sierra Leone
http://dx.doi.org/10.1596/978-1-4648-0742-8

highest among residents of Freetown, youth, men, and individuals with tertiary degrees. While wage workers have less control over their hours and are thus more often underemployed, the self-employed also work less than they desire, likely reflecting weak demand or other constraints to the expansion of business activities.

There is significant inequality in earnings across subgroups, but inactivity contributes most to household income poverty. Earnings vary substantially across job types and, within job type, across gender and educational attainment. Jobs in mining, Freetown, and private sector wage employment provide the highest earnings. Gender gaps in earnings are stark: holding other characteristics constant, the results show that men earn nearly three times as much as women in wage employment, more than 2.5 times in nonfarm self-employment, and nearly double in agricultural self-employment. Among people in wage or agricultural self-employment, there are large earnings gaps between individuals with tertiary education and individuals with less education. However, employment is more closely associated with income poverty than skills, job type, sector of activity, or even earnings while employed. Inequality across household incomes is also high, while the coverage of programs to help the most vulnerable access job opportunities is limited.

Skills

Educational attainment and literacy rates among the working-age population are low, and there are large differences by gender and location (figure ES.2). More than half the working-age population (56.7 percent) cannot read or write. A similar proportion have never attended school, and, among these, almost all are illiterate. Financial constraints are the main reason cited among those who have never attended school. Most (about 8 of 10 individuals) have attained, at most,

Figures ES.2 Literacy Rates, by Gender and Location

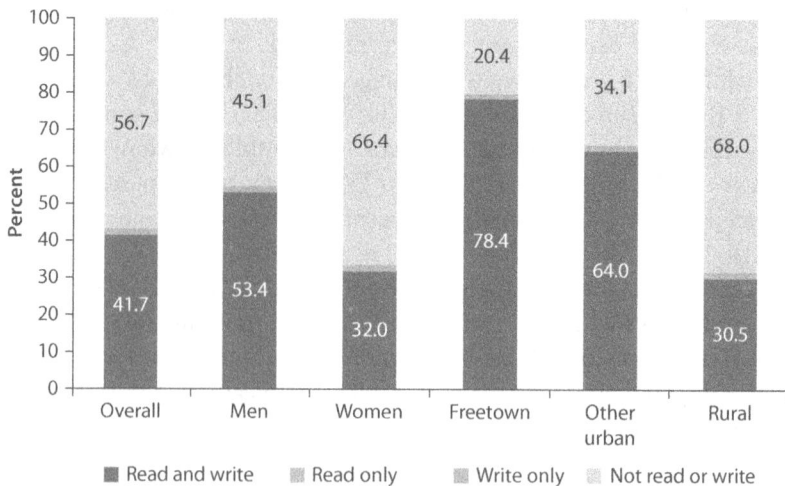

primary education, while only a small fraction have completed higher education. There are large gender gaps in both the illiteracy rate and the proportion of people who have never attended school. Educational attainment and literacy rates among the working-age population largely mirror the urban–rural distribution. Individuals in Freetown are the most well educated and literate, followed by residents in other urban areas, and, lastly, residents in rural areas. Most individuals are educated at public institutions; a relatively small proportion pursue training or apprenticeships.

Higher skill levels are associated with higher earnings, but most of the variation is at the tails of the distribution. There is a large jump in earnings among people with some primary relative to those with no schooling, and, similarly, among for those with postsecondary education relative to those who have completed secondary education. However, in the middle of the education spectrum, the returns to education do not vary much. To see earnings gains from vocational training, participants must obtain certificates or diplomas; there is no significant boost to median earnings associated with serving apprenticeships.

Farming and Nonfarm Household Enterprises

The majority of households and those employed within them are engaged in agricultural activities, and women constitute a larger share than men among these workers. Most households (72.8 percent) include at least one household member involved in agricultural activities, and about half of all households (49.6 percent) include at least one member engaged in a nonfarm household enterprise. A nonnegligible proportion of households and individuals diversify labor across farm and nonfarm self-employment (22.6 percent and 26.1 percent of those in nonfarm work, respectively). In both farm and nonfarm self-employment, women represent a larger share of the employed (53.5 percent and 63.8 percent, respectively). However, in terms of hours worked, men carry a larger burden of agricultural activities relative to women.

Educational attainment is lower among people working in agricultural self-employment than among the overall population and the nonfarm self-employed. Most of the agricultural self-employed (80 percent) never attended school, compared with 67.5 percent of the overall working-age population and 59.9 percent of the nonfarm self-employed. The vast majority of household enterprise workers (85.6 percent) work in enterprises that do not keep financial records for the business separate from the financial records for the household, indicating low financial literacy.

Capital—typically sourced from family and friends—is a key constraint on the quantity and quality of jobs among household enterprises (figure ES.3). Nearly half (47 percent) of household enterprises report that they are unable to borrow the necessary capital for the business. The initial level of capital invested in household enterprises is positively related to enterprise size, revenues, and

Figure ES.3 Source of Capital (% of Household Enterprises)

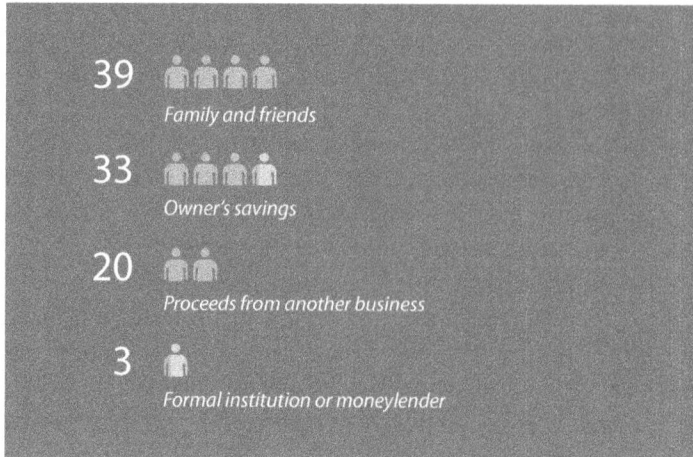

profits, indicating difficulties in obtaining capital may be limiting firm growth and productivity. Among those households able to borrow, start-up capital tends to be obtained from family and friends (40 percent); little capital is obtained from formal financial institutions (3 percent), pointing to incomplete credit markets. Credit constraints are also associated with more variable enterprise locations; variable locations are common (affecting 42.1 percent of household enterprises), but may further limit investments, for example, if assets cannot be properly secured.

Capital is also a key constraint to increased productivity in agricultural self-employment (figure ES.4). Almost 40 percent of agricultural workers live in households that face credit constraints, which are associated with less use of technology, inputs, extension services, and, ultimately, output, and profits. More than half of plots (63.9 percent) have no irrigation and do not use fertilizer (65.5 percent), and only 4.6 percent of agricultural workers belong to households that have access to extension services for farming activities. While more than half of plots (69.2 percent) use purchased seeds, the data suggest that capital constraints may be preventing households from investing in more productive, costlier inputs that could, in the absence of these constraints, increase income.

There are notable gender gaps in land and business ownership and in the resulting profits. Most agricultural plots (67.8 percent) are owned by men, and women typically own smaller plots (8.3 acres vs. 11.1 acres). In terms of household enterprises, although most are microenterprises, men tend to own slightly larger enterprises relative to women and are more likely than women to hire labor. And, although women are concentrated in nonfarm self-employment activities, male-owned enterprises have median monthly profits that are almost double those of female-owned enterprises.

Figures ES.4　Capital Constraints and Access to Agricultural Inputs and Services

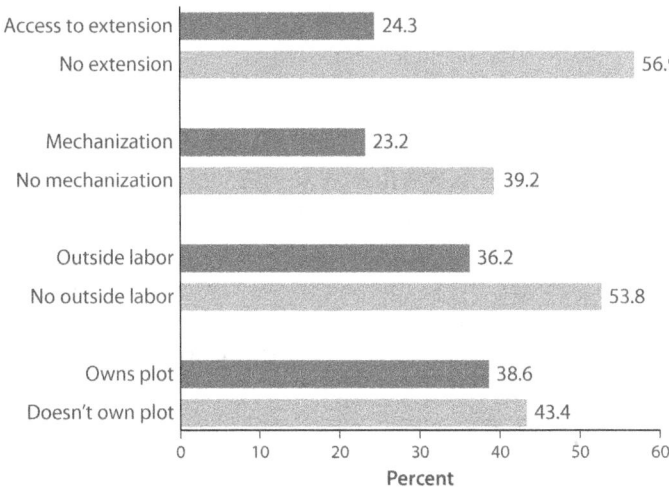

Informality

Informality is pervasive in Sierra Leone, and formal work is restricted to the few most highly educated workers. Over 35 percent of wage jobs and over 88 percent of nonagricultural self-employment are informal. The share of formal wage jobs is more than five times larger than the share of jobs in registered household enterprises involved in nonagricultural self-employment. Among wage workers, formal wage jobs are considered good jobs because these workers earn more, on average, than informal wage workers. The likelihood of working in a formal job, whether in wage employment or nonagricultural self-employment, is greater among men than among women and increases with educational attainment. Wage jobs in agriculture are almost never formal.

Youth

Youth—who represent the majority of the working-age population—participate less in the labor market and fare worse in terms of employment and unemployment. Youth (the 15–35 age group) represent the largest share of the overall population (66 percent) and more than half the employed population (56 percent). Relative to older people (36–64 age group), the share of youth both in the labor force and among the employed is much smaller, about a 30 percentage point difference relative to the older group. A significant portion of this difference arises because many youth are still in school and not simultaneously working. The unemployment rate is also higher among youth than among older people (5.9 percent versus 2.2 percent). The highest unemployment rate across subgroups occurs among young men (7.7 percent), particularly those who live in Freetown (14.0 percent). On the other hand, the differences in the type of job and the sector of employment are not large between youth and older people; most youth work in low-productivity jobs.

Findings from the 2014 Labor Force Survey in Sierra Leone
http://dx.doi.org/10.1596/978-1-4648-0742-8

Youth have higher literacy and more educational attainment relative to previous generations, but, otherwise, seem to acquire skills in a similar way. Literacy rates and educational attainment are higher among youth than among older people in the working-age population (photo ES.1). The skill composition among youth varies across districts and provinces, but the Western Area leads in terms of years of education. The proportion of youth engaging in vocational training and apprenticeships is similar to the proportion among the overall working-age population. There is a drop-off in average years of vocational training and apprenticeships among older age groups of youth, implying a trend among younger cohorts to stay in school longer. However, the fact that average years of schooling fluctuates around age 24 may reflect the impact of the civil conflict on human capital accumulation among people of school age during the war.

Gender gaps in educational attainment persist among youth, but are smaller than the corresponding gaps among older generations. Young women have an average of around 7 months less education than young men. Girls tend to leave school at slightly earlier ages than boys, and high rates of teenage pregnancy are likely reinforcing these gender gaps: among young women, 66.5 percent had their first child between the ages of 15 and 19. However, the necessity to start working also plays a role because young girls also begin working in almost equal proportion after they exit school.

Photo ES.1.   A young man supervises the transport of heavy machinery to Kono

Photo Credit: Andrea Martin.

Notes

1. This refers to the share of unemployed (that is, the total unemployed divided by the total working-age population), while the unemployment rate (4.3 percent) is calculated as the total unemployed divided by the total workforce (working-age population unemployed plus employed, excluding those who do not participate in the labor market).

2. See "Indicators on job types and main sectors" in the Appendix for details on how job types are defined.

3. Those who were not working but were available for work are referred to as "broad unemployment," to distinguish from the ILO definition of unemployment, which requires an individual to actively search to be considered unemployed.

Introduction

In Sierra Leone, where more than half of the population is poor and dependent on earnings from labor income, jobs are critical for poverty reduction and inclusive growth.[1] In 2011, 53 percent of the country's population of 5.9 million was living under the poverty line, and 14 percent was living under the food poverty line. Most workers, but especially the poorest, are engaged in low-productivity jobs in agriculture or nonagricultural self-employment. In a context of limited social safety nets and social insurance coverage, jobs remain the primary source of income among the poor and are therefore crucial to poverty reduction.[2]

The country's demographic profile implies that substantial job creation will be needed in coming years. According to the most recent United Nations population estimates, almost half of the population is below age 15, and more than three-quarters are below age 35 (figure I.1). At current rates of population growth, this implies new jobs will have to be created for approximately 100,000 labor market entrants per year.

At the same time, the sectors contributing the most to recent growth are traditionally low in labor intensity, adding to the jobs challenge. Since the end of a 10-year-long civil war in 2002 and prior to the Ebola Virus Disease crisis, the economy consistently registered positive growth. The average annual per capita growth was 5.8 percent between 2003 and 2011. However, the mining sector, driven by iron ore exports, represented 98.2 percent of the growth in gross domestic product (GDP) in 2014, while agriculture, which accounted for most of the country's labor, represented only 0.3 percent.

Creating jobs and improving the quality of jobs are vital to poverty reduction. Sierra Leone's current Poverty Reduction Strategy Paper, "The Agenda for Prosperity," identifies employment quality as a major driver of sustainable economic growth. However, robust economic growth since the country emerged from a decades-long civil war in 2002 has not translated into a corresponding increase in adequate, productive employment opportunities. Policy making around jobs should therefore consider not only the quantity but also the quality of jobs.

In Sierra Leone, as a postconflict country, jobs are also central to sustained stability. Internationally, there is a growing recognition that jobs are central to restoring peace and stability after conflict. Recent World Development Reports

Figure I.1   Population Pyramid, 2015 Estimate

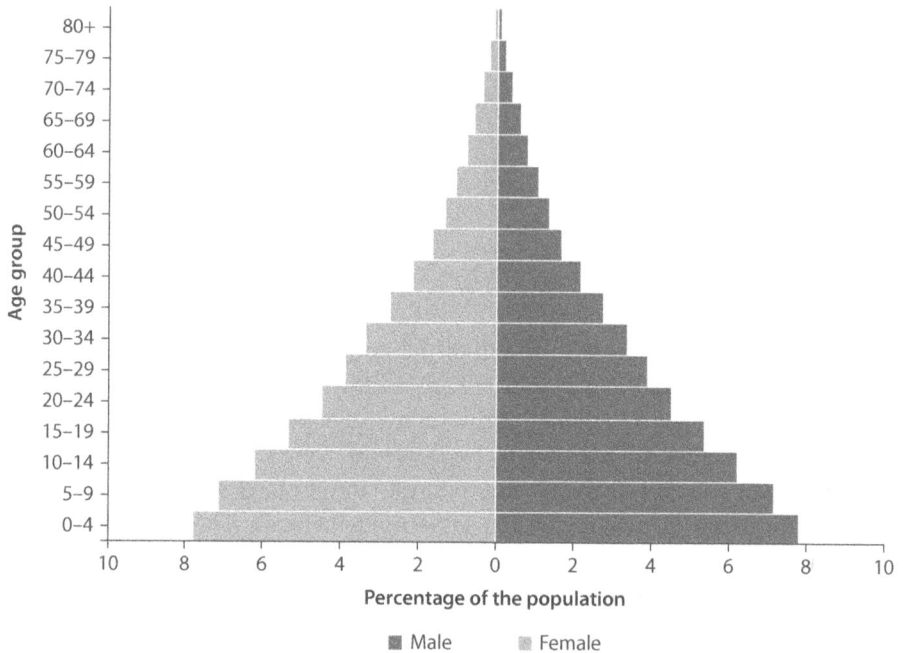

Source: United Nations Population Division, World Population Prospects, 2015.

have identified jobs as one of the most pressing issues in fragile and postconflict states. The 2011 report, on conflict, security, and development, identified jobs, alongside security and justice, as a central pillar for breaking the cycle of violence, restoring confidence in public institutions, and giving people a stake in society. Building on this, the 2013 report, on jobs, finds that both because of their contributions to livelihoods and poverty reduction and for reasons of social cohesion jobs can provide alternatives to violence, especially among youth.

Yet, despite the importance of jobs, the design of policies and interventions to promote opportunities for employment in Sierra Leone has been constrained by a limited knowledge base. Previously, the main source of employment statistics was the 2004 and 2011 Sierra Leone Integrated Household Surveys, which contained limited information on the labor force. To help fill this important knowledge gap, Statistics Sierra Leone, with the support of the World Bank, the ILO, and the Deutsche Gesellschaft für Internationale Zusammenarbeit, designed and implemented the 2014 Sierra Leone Labor Force Survey (SLLFS).

This report, relying on the first labor force survey in the country in almost 30 years, provides a picture of the jobs landscape in Sierra Leone. Data from the SLLFS, the first labor force survey in the country since 1984, were collected between July and August 2014 and constitute a nationally representative sample.[3] The SLLFS covered 4,200 households, representing more than 20,000 individuals. It contains a wealth of information on labor market activities, including detailed data on household enterprises and agricultural activities, and provides a more complete view of productive activities in Sierra Leone than would be possible with only a traditional labor force survey approach. This report uses concepts defined by the ILO to ensure international comparability, with adjustments, as needed, to contextual specificities. It also broadly aligns with the analytical framework of the 2013 World Development Report on Jobs and the Africa regional flagship on youth employment.

The report is divided into five sections. The first section provides an overview of the employment situation in Sierra Leone, ranging from labor force participation to the types of employment among the working-age population. The second section addresses issues related to skills (education, training, and apprenticeships). The third section discusses self-employment in agricultural activities and household enterprises, which are, respectively, the first- and second-largest sources of jobs in the economy. The fourth section considers informality in both wage employment and nonagricultural self-employment. The fifth section focuses on youth employment, using both the ILO definition (under age 25) and the definition generally used in the Africa region (15–35). The final section summarizes the results and provides policy recommendations.

Notes

1. The source of information in this section is the Sierra Leone Poverty Assessment (2013) unless otherwise indicated.
2. World Bank, 2012, Sierra Leone Social Protection Assessment.
3. The response rate was 99.7 percent, resulting in a final total of 4,189 households, corresponding to 20,378 individuals. As is the common practice with survey data, the data are then weighted to represent the entire population of the country.

CHAPTER 1

Overview

This chapter presents a description of the overall labor market in Sierra Leone. It comprises three parts: a characterization of the labor market as a whole, an analysis of the employed based on the characteristics of their main employment at the time of the survey, and an analysis of the unemployed. Employment is decomposed into three broad types: wage employment, agricultural self-employment, and nonagricultural self-employment (photo 1.1). Self-employment can include employers or workers in household enterprises who share in profits. Salaried individuals in household enterprises are considered wage workers. Each of these job types is further decomposed by educational attainment, gender, disability status, migrant or nonmigrant status, and location in rural or urban areas and in government administrative area.[1] Table 1.1 presents the headline statistics that underlie the discussion.[2] The employment section discusses the relevant shares of people and their earnings.

The Overall Labor Market

In a working-age population of slightly more than 3 million people, 62.2 percent are employed.[3] According to the ILO definition of employment, this includes everyone who worked in the production of goods or services for pay or profit at least an hour during the calendar week preceding the interview. It also includes individuals temporarily absent from work because of health issues, vacation, or maternity or paternity leave; individuals who are away from work for less than a month or from one to three months; and individuals still receiving pay, while not working. Individuals who worked producing goods or services exclusively for household consumption are not considered employed in the ILO definition, nor are individuals who do not work for pay or profit. If any part of a household's production is sold, work in agriculture is considered employment under the ILO definition.

Over 9 percent of the working-age population was not employed and was available for work, but only one-third of these were actively looking for work.

Photo 1.1 A fisherman in Bonthe prepares to cast his net

Photo Credit: Hector Zamora.

This implies that 2.8 percent of the working-age population was unemployed under the ILO definition (unemployed, available, and looking); the remainder of those not employed, though available, were in broad unemployment (unemployed, available, but not looking). Not all people who are not working are available for work:.some are in school; others may be at home fulfilling responsibilities such as child or elderly care; and still others may be disabled and unable to participate in the labor market. Among people without jobs who are available to work, there may be many reasons why they are not looking for work (see section "Unemployment").

Combining the employed and the unemployed results in a labor force participation rate of 65.0 percent and 71.3 percent, based on the ILO definition or the broader definition of unemployment, respectively.[4] The remaining people are out of the labor force, implying an inactivity rate of 35.0 percent under the ILO definition and 28.7 under the broader definition. Of the working-age population, 6.4 percent are not working and are available for work, though they are not actively searching.

Labor force participation varies widely by educational attainment, but much less across population subgroups defined otherwise than by education. Over 80.0 percent of the most well educated participate in the labor market, whereas the share is only 44.2 percent among those who have only completed primary school. By contrast, the difference in participation rates between men and women is small (only 1.2 percentage points lower among women), as are the

Table 1.1 Key Aggregate Labor Market Statistics

	Employed (%)	Unemployed (ILO) (%)	Unemployed (broad) (%)	Working-age population	Workforce (ILO definition)	Labor force participation (ILO) (%)	Unemployment rate (ILO) (%)
Overall	62.2	2.8	9.1	3,009,472	1,956,912	65.0	4.3
Youth (AFR)	52.4	3.3	10.1	1,988,575	1,108,067	55.7	5.9
Men	62.4	3.3	8.4	1,367,915	898,394	65.7	5.0
Women	62.1	2.4	9.7	1,641,557	1,058,518	64.5	3.7
Disabled	63.1	0.9	2.7	82,172	52,573	64.0	1.4
Not disabled	62.2	2.8	9.3	2,927,299	1,904,339	65.1	4.4
Migrant	61.2	3.6	8.5	459,684	297,785	64.8	5.6
Not migrant	62.5	2.7	9.2	2,537,514	1,653,187	65.1	4.1
Never went to school	76.1	2.1	9.1	1,660,372	1,297,325	78.1	2.6
Incomplete primary	50.1	3.4	10.6	227,620	121,889	53.5	6.4
Completed primary	41.5	2.8	7.4	421,769	186,606	44.2	6.3
Completed lower secondary	42.2	2.9	7.2	382,090	172,534	45.2	6.5
Completed upper secondary	43.7	5.1	11.9	250,002	121,885	48.8	10.5
Tech degrees + certificates	74.2	9.8	15.5	50,167	42,146	84.0	11.7
Tertiary degree	75.1	8.2	11.6	17,451	14,527	83.2	9.8
Urban freetown	47.9	6.0	12.0	344,326	185,711	53.9	11.1
Other urban	50.4	3.6	7.9	514,825	278,381	54.1	6.7
Rural	67.3	2.1	8.9	2,150,320	1,492,820	69.4	3.0
Eastern	63.8	2.0	7.3	685,102	451,230	65.9	3.1
Northern	69.5	2.8	8.9	1,154,417	834,965	72.3	3.9
Southern	56.7	1.9	9.5	788,008	462,119	58.6	3.2
Western Area	48.8	5.8	12.1	381,944	208,599	54.6	10.7

Source: 2014 Sierra Leone Labor Force Survey.
Note: The column Employed corresponds to the total employed, divided by the working-age population; the column Unemployed (ILO) corresponds to the unemployed (according to the ILO definition), divided by the working-age population, but the column Unemployment Rate (ILO) corresponds to the unemployed (ILO), divided by the workforce (ILO). Hence, Employed + Unemployed (ILO) = Labor force participation (ILO). Because of missing information, some individuals could not be assigned to a subpopulation (for example, migrants). In these cases, the sum of the subpopulations is less than the overall population, and the statistics for these subpopulations refer to individuals who report the information; individuals on whom data are missing are excluded from the calculations.

differences by disability status (the participation rate is 1.1 percentage points lower among the disabled than among the nondisabled) and migration status (the participation rate is 0.5 percentage points lower among migrants than among nonmigrants).

Labor force participation increases rapidly with age (figure 1.1). Labor force participation is 55.7 percent among youth (15–35 age group) and 34.8 percent among youth defined according to the ILO definition (15–24 age group); the rest are out of the labor force, and many are still in school (see chapter 5). Labor force participation averages 85.1 percent among prime-age workers (36–55 age group), but is only 75.3 percent among the elderly of working age (55–64 age group).

Labor force participation varies across geographical areas and is lower in urban areas (map 1.1). The participation rate is 53.9 percent in urban Freetown and 54.1 percent in other urban areas, compared with the considerably higher rate of 69.4 percent in rural areas. The participation rate in Northern Province is the highest: 72.3 percent of the working-age population is either employed or unemployed (ILO), while Southern Province and the Western Area have the lowest participation rates and consequently the highest inactivity rates (41.4 and 45.4 percent are inactive, respectively). Eastern Province is in the middle: the participation rate is 65.9 percent. Inactivity rates across districts run as high as 46.7 percent, in Bo, and as low as 20.6 percent, in Tonkolili. The Western Area Urban District has a relatively low participation rate, 53.8 percent, but other

Figure 1.1 Labor Force Participation Rates (ILO), by Age

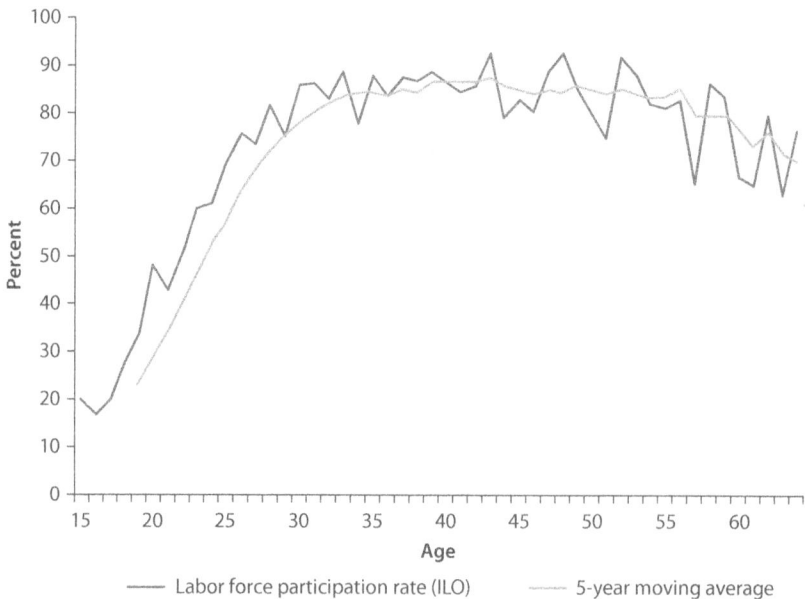

Source: 2014 Sierra Leone Labor Force Survey.

Map 1.1 Labor Force Participation Rates (ILO), by District

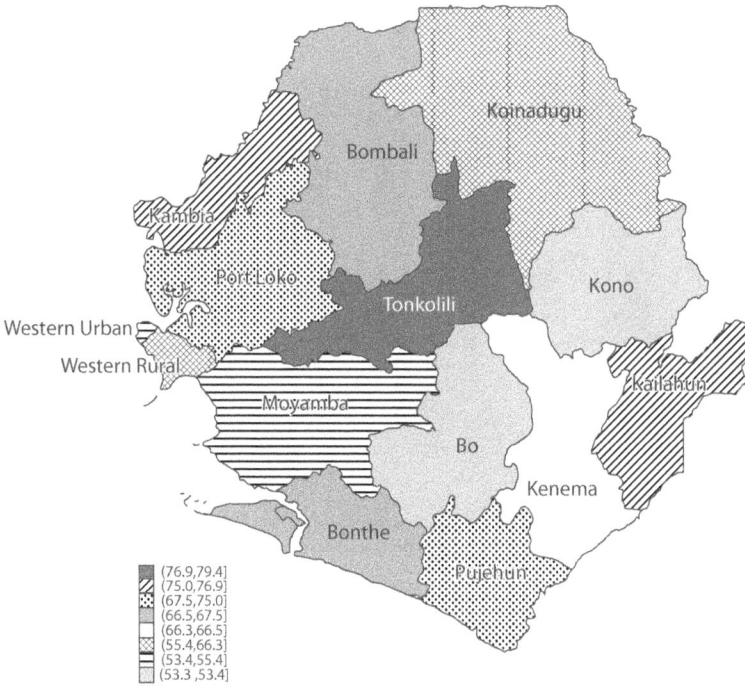

Legend	
▨	(76.9,79.4]
▧	(75.0,76.9]
▨	(67.5,75.0]
▨	(66.5,67.5]
▨	(66.3,66.5]
▨	(55.4,66.3]
▤	(53.4,55.4]
▢	(53.3 ,53.4]

Source: 2014 Sierra Leone Labor Force Survey.

relatively urbanized districts such as Kenema (26.8 percent urban) show higher participation rates (66.4 percent).

Statistical analysis of the determinants of the labor market highlights these results, as well as several additional factors (see appendix B). For example, men, individuals with postsecondary degrees, younger workers, and urban residents (including urban Freetown) are significantly more likely to be unemployed than, respectively, women, the less well educated, older workers, and rural residents. Women are significantly more likely to be out of the labor force, as are the disabled, people with upper-secondary degrees (and, to a lesser extent, people with lower-secondary degrees), younger people, and urban residents.

The main reason for inactivity is attendance at school or in training programs, especially among urban residents and men (figure 1.2). Taking care of the home or family affects women much more than men, reflecting important gender differences in the division of household chores. The lack of financial resources to start a new business is a more powerful reason among nonmigrants than among migrants (17.4 percent vs. 9.1 percent) and among rural residents than among urban dwellers (45.4 percent vs. 69 percent).

Over two-thirds of the inactive in the Western Area report the main reason they are not participating in the labor market is that they are in school or

Figure 1.2 Reasons for Inactivity, by Characteristics of Individuals

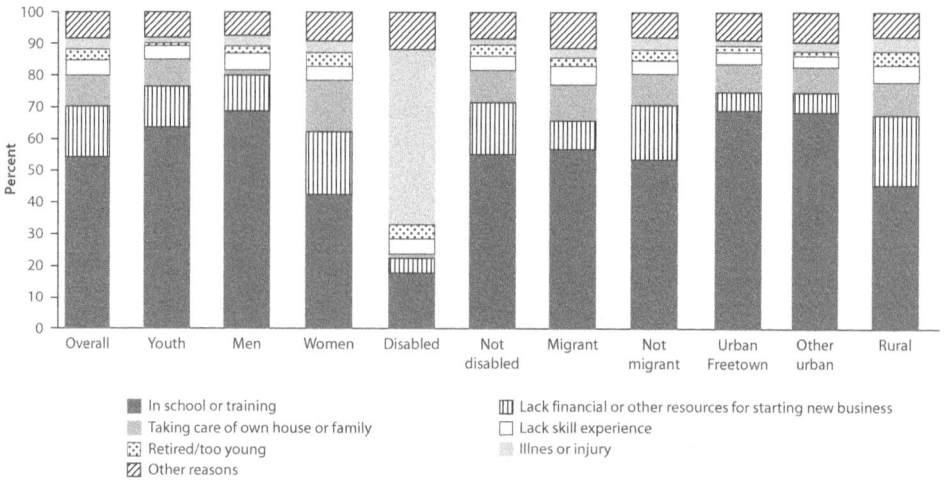

Source: 2014 Sierra Leone Labor Force Survey.
Note: "Other reasons" in figure 1.2 and figure 1.3 include waiting for replies to inquiries, does not want to work, disabled, discouraged, off-season, pregnant, transportation problems, waiting to start new job or business, and so on.

Figure 1.3 Reasons for Inactivity, by Province and Educational Attainment

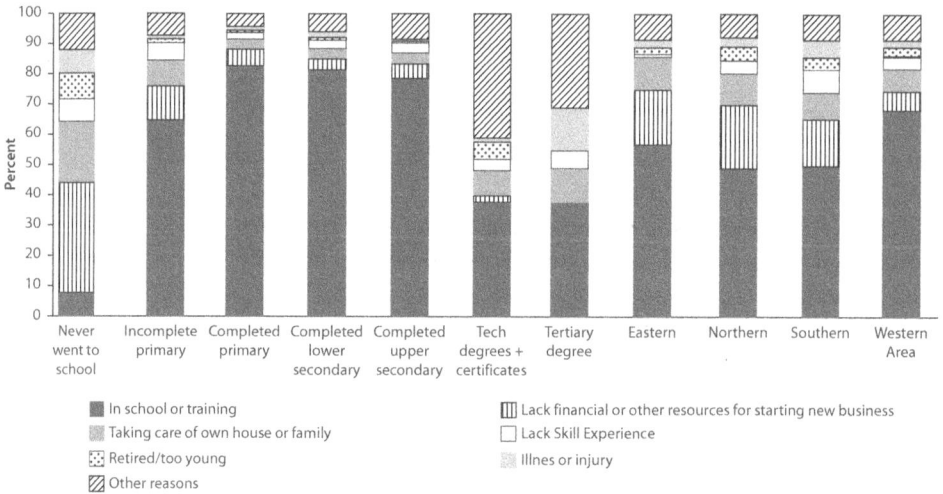

Source: 2014 Sierra Leone Labor Force Survey.

undergoing training (figure 1.3). The reason given for not participating in the labor market by people who have some education, but who have not reached higher levels of education (technical degrees, certificates, or tertiary degrees), mostly revolves around attendance at school or in training programs.[5] Lacking financial or other resources to start a new business and taking care of the home or family are cited disproportionately by people who have never attended school relative to people with some educational attainment.

Employment

The share of the working-age population that is actually employed varies greatly across the country (map 1.2). Tonkolili District, where 77.2 percent of the working-age population is in employment, has the highest employment-to-population ratio, and Kailahun (76.2 percent) and Kambia (75.6 percent) districts are not far behind.[6] At the other end of the spectrum, the Western Area Urban District (47.8 percent), Kono (50.9 percent), Moyamba (52.5 percent), and Bo (52.5 percent) have the lowest employment rates. Although unemployment rates and the employment-to-population ratio are highly (negatively) correlated (−0.665), variations in labor force participation can also affect employment rates.

Employment can be characterized by the type of job and the sector of employment activity. This report considers self-employment, decomposed into agricultural and nonagricultural self-employment, and wage and salary employment among possible job types.[7] Unpaid labor is also considered a type of job, although it is not considered employment by the ILO. The sectors of employment are agriculture, fishing, and forestry; mining and extractive industries; manufacturing and utilities; construction; and services. A summary of key employment statistics using these decompositions is presented in table 1.2.

Map 1.2 The Employment-to-Population Ratio

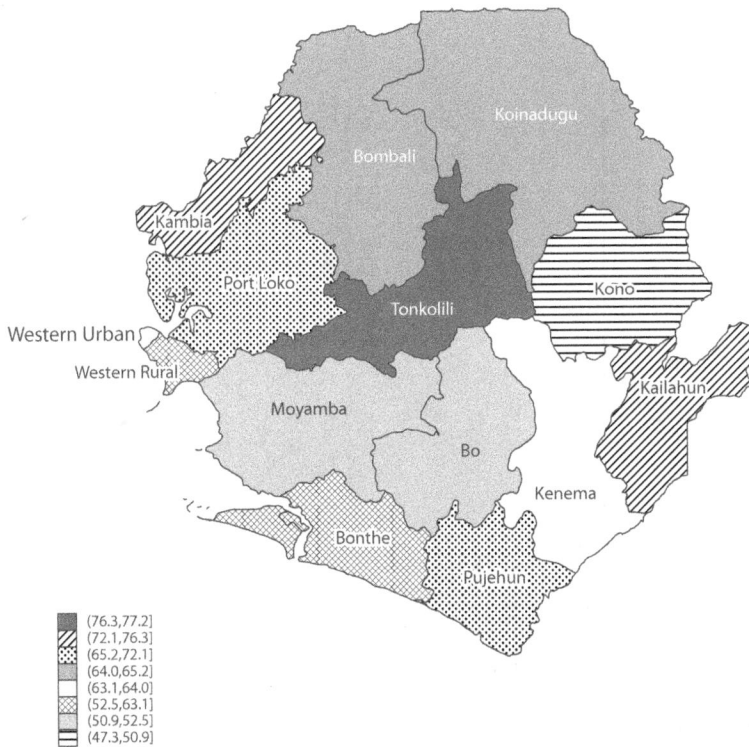

[76.3,77.2]
[72.1,76.3]
[65.2,72.1]
[64.0,65.2]
[63.1,64.0]
[52.5,63.1]
[50.9,52.5]
[47.3,50.9]

Source: 2014 Sierra Leone Labor Force Survey.

Findings from the 2014 Labor Force Survey in Sierra Leone
http://dx.doi.org/10.1596/978-1-4648-0742-8

Table 1.2 Key Employment Statistics

	Agricultural Self-Employment (%)	Nonagricultural Self-Employment (%)	Wage Employment (%)	Unpaid Labor[a] (%)	Agriculture, Fishing and Forestry (%)	Mining and Extractive Industries (%)	Manufacturing and Utilities (%)	Construction (%)	Services (%)
Overall	59.2	31.3	9.5	6.5	61.1	1.5	2.8	1.2	33.4
Youth (AFR)	58.8	31.9	9.3	7.5	61.1	1.2	3.1	1.3	33.2
Men	59.7	24.8	15.5	6.6	62.2	3.0	5.6	2.7	26.6
Women	58.7	36.8	4.5	6.4	60.1	0.2	0.5	0.1	39.2
Disabled	61.9	30.7	7.5	6.6	62.5	0.1	4.6	0.6	32.2
Not disabled	59.1	31.4	9.6	6.5	61.0	1.5	2.8	1.3	33.4
Migrant	27.0	48.3	24.7	4.3	28.8	5.4	3.5	3.3	59.0
Not migrant	64.9	28.4	6.8	6.9	66.6	0.8	2.7	0.9	29.0
Never went to school	69.8	27.7	2.5	6.5	71.4	1.3	1.7	0.7	24.9
Incomplete primary	52.4	40.4	7.2	8.5	54.5	1.9	4.5	1.4	37.6
Completed primary	47.8	41.5	10.7	9.3	50.9	1.3	6.7	2.6	38.5
Completed lower secondary	35.0	44.8	20.2	5.5	37.7	1.8	4.9	1.8	53.8
Completed upper secondary	21.8	36.9	41.4	3.1	23.5	2.5	4.6	3.6	65.8
Tech degrees + certificates	9.0	17.0	74.1	1.6	8.8	1.2	2.9	3.2	83.9
Tertiary degree	0.0	10.3	89.7	0.0	1.3	1.7	0.3	2.3	94.3
Urban freetown	0.5	59.0	40.5	2.6	0.6	0.1	6.5	6.1	86.6
Other urban	21.3	56.8	21.8	5.1	24.0	4.1	4.3	2.1	65.6
Rural	72.9	23.5	3.6	7.1	74.4	1.1	2.2	0.5	21.7
Eastern	71.8	22.5	5.6	3.3	72.5	3.1	1.9	1.1	21.4
Northern	66.5	28.9	4.6	6.1	67.7	0.3	2.7	0.8	28.5
Southern	56.7	32.9	10.4	11.8	61.5	2.4	2.5	0.4	33.1
Western Area	3.4	59.2	37.5	2.4	3.6	0.2	6.1	5.7	84.4

Source: 2014 Sierra Leone Labor Force Survey.

Note: Because of missing information, some individuals could not be assigned to a subpopulation. In these cases, the sum of the subpopulations is less than the overall population, and the statistics on these subpopulations refer to individuals who report the information; individuals on whom data are missing are excluded from the calculations.

a. Unpaid labor is not considered employment in the ILO definitions; so, the shares of job types among ILO-recognized employment (agricultural and nonagricultural self-employment and wage employment) sums to 100 percent. The data on unpaid labor represent the number of unpaid workers as a percentage of the total number of employed (ILO) workers.

Job Types

Most workers are self-employed or employed in farming or household enterprises, while few earn wages or salaries in exchange for their labor. The vast majority of workers (91.0 percent) are self-employed: 59.2 percent in agricultural self-employment, and around one-third (31.3 percent) in nonagricultural self-employment, while only 9.5 percent are wage workers. This is consistent with the above-mentioned results indicating that employment rates are higher in rural areas than in urban areas and are roughly comparable with rates in other countries in Sub-Saharan Africa, although the share in wage labor is slightly lower, and the share in nonagricultural self-employment is slightly higher.[8] Moreover, if most individuals consider the norm to be self-employment rather than wage employment, it is not surprising that (broad) unemployed workers are far more concerned about access to capital (needed to start a self-employment venture) than about the availability of jobs (implying wage employment), as suggested in section "Reasons Not to Search for Work".

Education is a key determinant of the type of job a person occupies. Nearly 90 percent of employed individuals with tertiary degrees work in wage jobs; none of the interviewed individuals with tertiary degrees were working in agriculture or as unpaid labor. Conversely, only 2.5 percent of the employed who have never attended school work in wage jobs, whereas 69.8 percent work in agricultural self-employment, and an additional 6.5 percent (relative to the total number of employed) are working without pay. Nonagricultural self-employment includes employed individuals at all levels of educational attainment, but this is particularly the case among individuals who started school, but did not continue beyond upper-secondary education. A relatively large share of workers with low educational attainment are in unpaid work: 9.3 percent of workers who have only completed primary school and 8.5 percent of workers who have some primary school, but have not completed it.

Most wage jobs are concentrated in urban areas and among certain demographic groups such as men and migrants. The majority (71 percent) of wage jobs are in Freetown and other urban areas. Beyond the obvious distributions of job types, with more agricultural employment in rural areas and less in the Western Area, there are less straightforward differences in the types of jobs among the various categories of the employed population. For example, if they have jobs, women are much less likely than men to be in wage employment (4.5 percent among women vs. 15.5 percent among men), but this gap is more than offset by the higher share of women in nonagricultural self-employment (36.8 percent vs. 24.8 percent among men). Employed migrant workers are much more likely than employed nonmigrant workers to be in wage jobs in part because, in nearly one-fifth of all cases, employed migrants have moved to the districts in which they had found wage work. Employed migrants are also significantly less likely to be in agricultural self-employment, a result largely linked to the fact that over 40 percent of migrants reside in the Western Area Urban District, where agricultural employment is practically nonexistent.

People who start out young in the labor force tend, as they become older, to end up in wage work and nonagricultural self-employment, but not in unpaid work (figure 1.4). Among the employed between 15 and 19 years of age, an average of 15.7 percent were primarily engaged in unpaid labor, while only 2.1 percent had wage jobs, and 24.0 percent were in nonagricultural self-employment. By ages 36–40, 8.9 percent had a wage job, 29.5 percent were in nonagricultural wage employment, and only 3.7 percent were working without pay. Agricultural self-employment remained relatively stable, averaging 58.2 percent of all jobs among 15–19-year-olds who were working and 57.9 percent among people 36–40 years old.

The types of jobs available and the use of unpaid labor also vary widely across districts (map 1.3). Agricultural self-employment is more prevalent in more rural districts such as Kailahun (93.0 percent of all jobs, 82.4 percent rural), Kambia (73.7 percent of jobs, 83.0 percent rural), and Tonkolili (79.3 percent of jobs, 91.3 percent rural). Perhaps, surprisingly, the highly rural districts of Moyamba (90.1 percent rural) and Koinadugu (93.1 percent rural) had relatively fewer agricultural self-employment jobs (60.9 percent and 60.7 percent, respectively) and a relatively large share of nonagricultural self-employment (34.9 percent and 31.4 percent, respectively). In the Western Area Urban District, most jobs (58.9 percent) are in nonagricultural self-employment, and wage employment makes up almost all the remainder (40.7 percent).

A statistical analysis of the determinants of job types confirms many of these conclusions.[9] The chances of occupying a wage job increase significantly with educational attainment, whereas the likelihood of working in nonagricultural self-employment decreases with education. Men are more likely than women to be wage employees or in nonagricultural self-employment and are even slightly more likely to be unpaid contributing family workers. Wage work is

Figure 1.4   Job Types, by Age

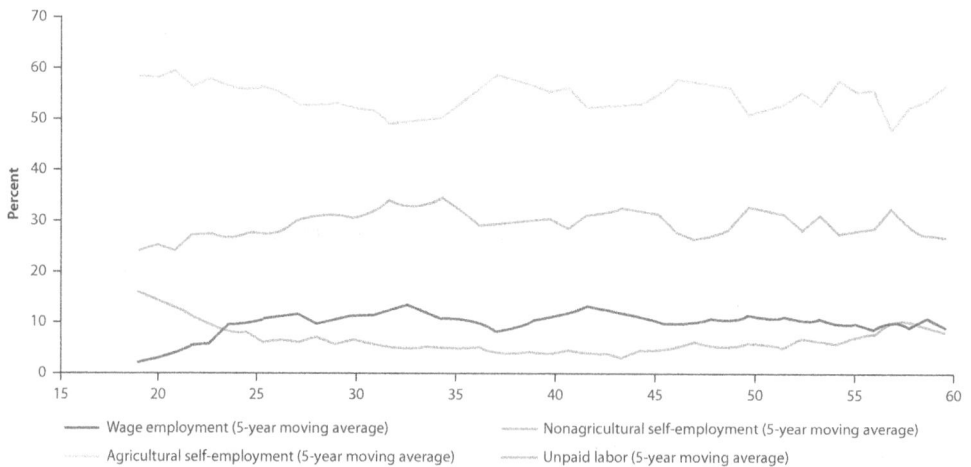

Source: 2014 Sierra Leone Labor Force Survey.

Map 1.3 Job Types, by District

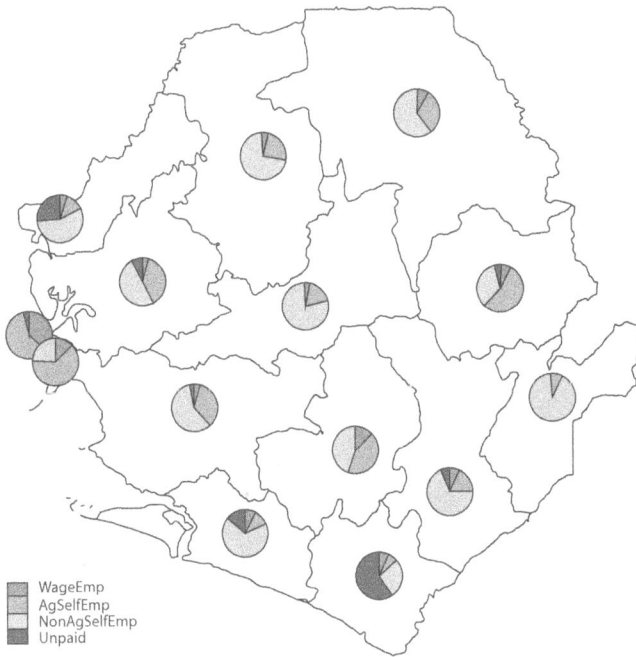

WageEmp
AgSelfEmp
NonAgSelfEmp
Unpaid

Source: 2014 Sierra Leone Labor Force Survey.

significantly more prevalent in Freetown and other urban areas than in rural areas, as is nonagricultural self-employment. The likelihood of being a wage worker or in nonagricultural self-employment increases with age up to the 30–34 age group, then decreases as people age. Wage work is more likely to be found in mining and, especially, manufacturing than in services and less likely to be found in agriculture.

Sector of Employment
Overall, the agricultural sector provides most jobs, with services the second most important source of jobs; mining makes only a minor contribution to jobs. The agricultural and services sectors provide 61.1 percent and 33.4 percent of all jobs, respectively. Although much attention has been paid to mining and extractive industries, this sector only provides 1.4 percent of all jobs, similar to the share provided by construction (1.2 percent). Although it supplies jobs to only 2.8 percent of the employed, manufacturing is a relatively crucial source of employment among people who started school, but never completed more than secondary school (as high as 6.6 percent of jobs among people who completed only primary school), men (5.5 percent), and urban dwellers (5.1 percent).

The relative importance of each sector varies dramatically across the country (map 1.4). As noted in section "Job Types," many rural districts are overwhelmingly focused on the agricultural sector (93 percent of jobs in Kailahun,

Map 1.4 Employment Sectors, by District

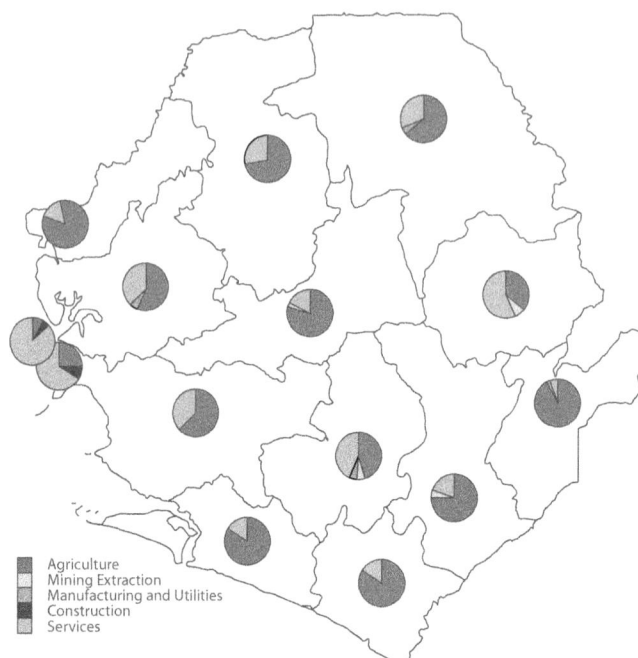

Agriculture
Mining Extraction
Manufacturing and Utilities
Construction
Services

Source: 2014 Sierra Leone Labor Force Survey.

79.3 percent in Tonkolili, and 73.7 percent in Kambia). The service sector is the provider of more jobs in more urban districts such as the districts in the Western Area (86.6 percent of jobs in the Western Area Urban District and 67.4 percent in the Western Area Rural District), Bo (45.1 percent of jobs), and Kono (53.7 percent). Jobs in the mining and extraction sector are mainly found in Kono (6.1 percent of employment), Bo (4.6 percent), and Kenema (4.1 percent), while manufacturing jobs are spread throughout the country, with the exception of Pujehun (0.7 percent of jobs), Bombali (0.9 percent), and Kambia (0.9 percent), where they are especially rare.

The vast majority of people working in the agricultural sector are self-employed, but the importance of self-employment in other sectors varies (table 1.3). Nearly all jobs in the agricultural sector (90.7 percent) are in self-employment. Jobs in the manufacturing and utilities sector are accounted for largely by the self-employed (71.9 percent), suggesting that unexploited economies of scale and opportunities for improving productivity may exist in this sector. Jobs in the service sector are largely accounted for by self-employment (77.6 percent), although it is less clear that the optimal scale of production in many services would require larger firms and more wage labor. Employment in the mining and construction sectors is more balanced between wage work and self-employment, but these sectors make up a small share of total employment in most districts, thus explaining the limited penetration of wage employment in the labor market.[10]

Table 1.3 Job Type, by Sector of Activity

Sector of activity	Agricultural self-employment (%)	Nonagricultural self-employment (%)	Wage employment (%)	Unpaid labor (%)
Agriculture, fishing and forestry	90.7	0.0	0.8	8.5
Mining and extractive industries	0.0	51.0	44.8	4.1
Manufacturing and utilities	0.0	71.9	19.1	9.0
Construction	0.0	46.0	52.9	1.1
Services	0.0	77.6	19.6	2.9

Source: 2014 Sierra Leone Labor Force Survey.

Type of Institution or Firm

The main economic activity of more than half the employed is work in private farming enterprises or farming cooperatives. Farming cooperatives and private farming enterprises employ 59.6 percent of all workers, and 87.0 percent of these farmworkers are agricultural self-employed (figure 1.5). Nonfarm cooperatives and private farming enterprises employ the second-largest share of workers (31.0 percent), and 79.0 percent of these nonfarm workers are nonagricultural self-employed. Local governments, the central government, public or state-owned enterprises, and parastatal institutions employ 4.2 percent of all workers.

Employment in the public sector and related sectors is relatively less prevalent, concentrated in the capital, and typically occupied by those with postsecondary educational attainment.[11] Around 5.0 percent of the employed work in the public sector, nongovernmental organizations (NGOs), or international organizations. Around 95.0 percent of the individuals who have never attended school and 84.8 percent of those who have completed lower-secondary education are working in a farm or nonfarm private enterprise or cooperative. Even among people who have completed upper-secondary education, nearly 70 percent are working in a farm or nonfarm private enterprise or cooperative. However, nearly half (49.6 percent) of people with technical degrees or certificates and over half (54.1 percent) of people with tertiary degrees are employed in the public sector. Furthermore, NGOs and international organizations represent a significant share of jobs for these workers, too (10.0 percent of those with technical degrees or certificates and 11.0 percent of those with tertiary degrees). The relative lack of opportunity among the most well-educated workers outside the public sector can be linked to the fragmented nature of the other sectors of the economy. Thus, among workers in farm enterprises or cooperative workers, only 0.8 percent are wage employees, and, among nonfarm household enterprise or cooperative workers, only 12.3 percent are wage employees. This suggests there is a lost potential in the private sector, given that the country's most well-educated workers are disproportionately diverted toward the public sector, NGOs, and international organizations and away from private sector employers.

Figure 1.5 Employment, by Type of Institution or Firm

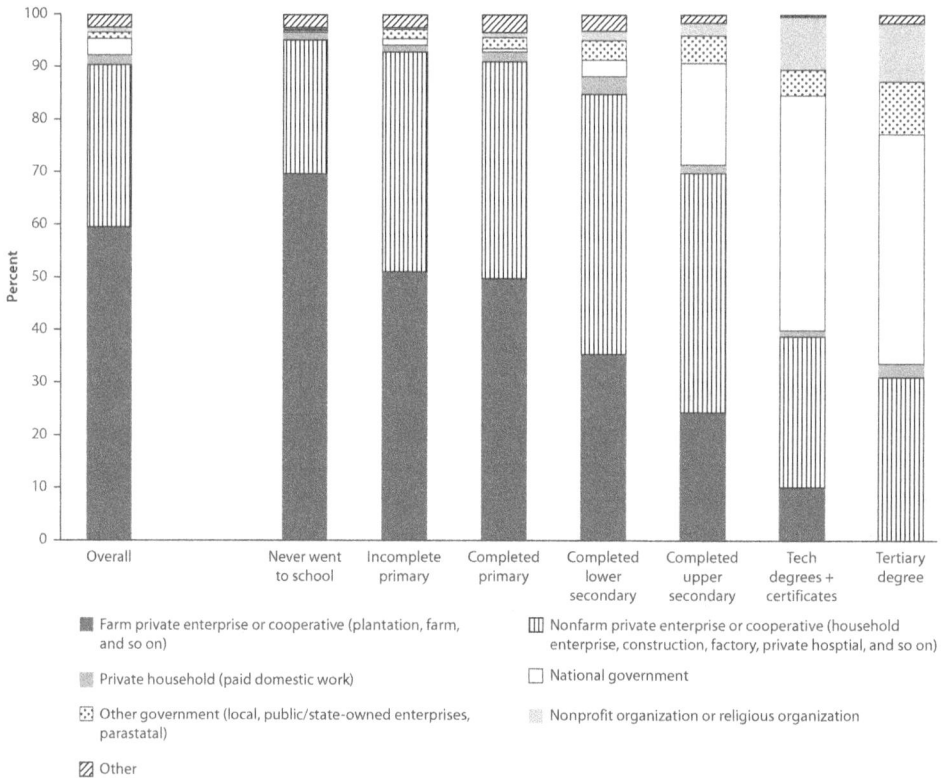

Source: 2014 Sierra Leone Labor Force Survey.

How the Employed Found Their Current Job

The employed tend to find jobs through family and friends, reflecting the importance of these ties in the labor market. Among employed individuals, the majority (62.8 percent) found their jobs through family members, friends, or acquaintances (figure 1.6). The second most common way to find a job is to launch or acquire a business. About one-fifth of the employed find jobs in this manner. Women are slightly more likely than men to rely on this channel (22.1 percent vs. 18.3 percent). Finding a job through family and friends and launching a business are more important strategies in rural than in urban areas.

Employed individuals with lower levels of educational attainment tend to have found their jobs through family and friends more often than the more highly educated (figure 1.7). Employed individuals who have never attended school have found jobs in this way 67.0 percent of the time, compared with 16.4 percent among the employed with tertiary degrees. The relative share of individuals who have jobs because they launched or acquired their own businesses also diminishes with education, which is a reflection of the larger proportion of

Figure 1.6   How the Employed Found Their Jobs, by Characteristics of Individuals

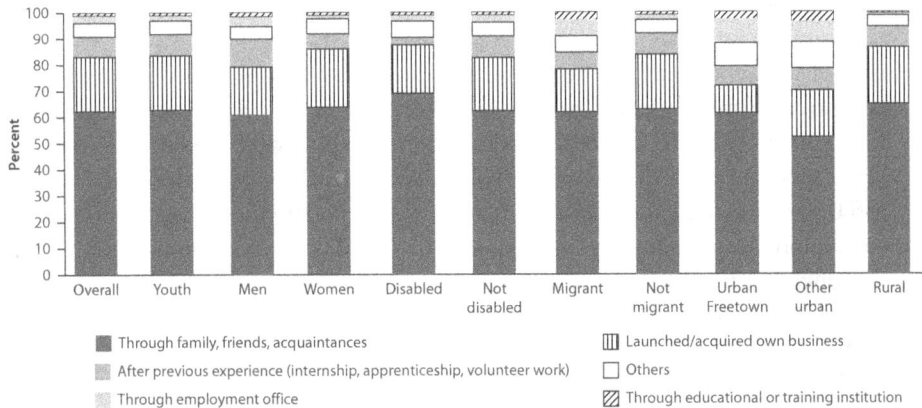

Source: 2014 Sierra Leone Labor Force Survey.
Note: The "Others" category includes direct inquiries with employers, advertisements, recruitments on the street, and so on.

Figure 1.7   How the Employed Found Their Jobs, by Educational Attainment and Province

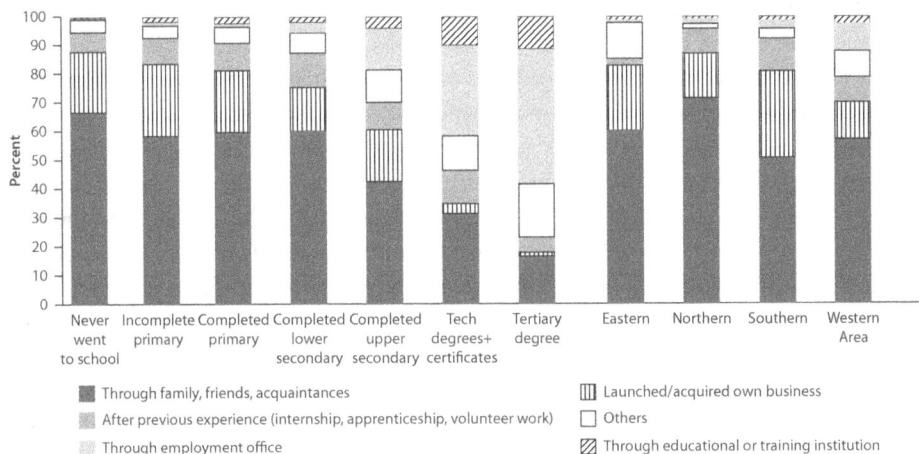

Source: 2014 Sierra Leone Labor Force Survey.
Note: The "Others" category includes direct inquiries with employers, advertisements in the press or on the Internet, recruitments on the street, and so on.

the wage employed among people with tertiary educational attainment and the larger proportion of the self-employed among people with low educational attainment. The share of the employed who have relied on employment offices to find jobs increases with educational attainment: it is only 0.3 percent among people who have never attended school, 4 percent among those who completed lower-secondary school, and 47.1 percent among those with tertiary degrees. This disparity could indicate that individuals with lower educational attainment do not know or have access to available employment services, but also likely reflects the scarcity of wage jobs and the prevalence of household enterprise and farming activities.

Underemployment

Almost one-third of all workers would like to work more hours, and this proportion is much larger in urban Freetown than in other areas. In Freetown, 47.0 percent of workers would like to work more hours, compared with 32.0 percent in
rural areas. Similarly, youth are a little more affected (35.0 percent) than others
(31.0 percent) by the desire to work more hours, but without success. A slightly
larger share of men than women would like to work more hours than they do
(36.0 percent vs. 31.0 percent). As the level of education increases, the desire to
work more hours than one does also rises, from 32.0 percent among people with
no education to 41.0 percent among people with tertiary degrees. This may be a
sign of the low capacity of the labor market to absorb more highly skilled people.

Nearly one-third of part-time workers (people who work less than 40 hours a
week) are working less than they would like (figure 1.8). The underemployment
rate is 30.9 percent and is higher among men (35 percent) than among women
(28.1 percent).[12] The underemployment rate is highest in the Western Area Urban
District and other urban areas. In urban Freetown, over half the people working
less than 8 hours a day are underemployed (51.1 percent), which is considerably
higher than the rate in rural areas (28.6 percent). The labor market in urban areas
appears to be less able to provide full-time jobs to those who desire them.

Although wage workers have less control over their hours and are thus more
often underemployed, the self-employed may also face weak demand or other
constraints, resulting in fewer hours worked than desired. As illustrated in
figure 1.9, 44.6 percent of all wage employees who work fewer than 8 hours a
week wish they could work more hours, which is considerably higher than the rate
among all people who work fewer than 8 hours a week. Among the nonagricultural self-employed, the underemployment rate is also high (35.9 percent) relative
to the overall underemployment rate. The lowest underemployment rate by job
type is among the agricultural self-employed, which is reasonable if one considers
that the hours worked are typically more flexible among the agricultural

Figure 1.8 Underemployment Rates, by Characteristics of Individuals

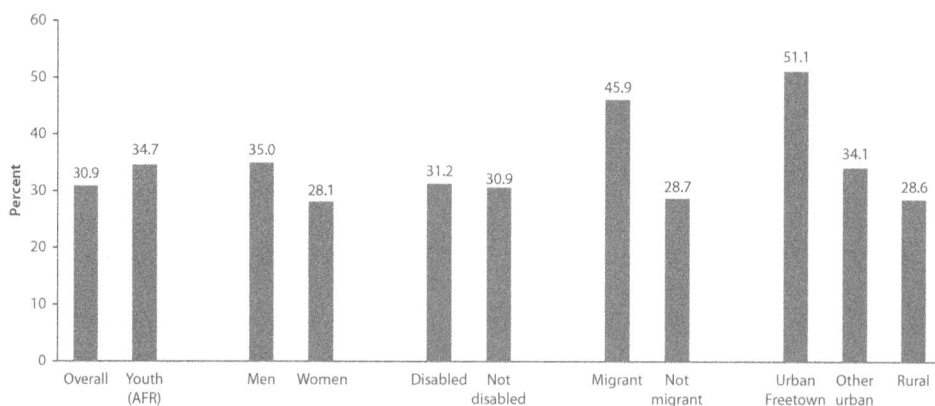

Source: 2014 Sierra Leone Labor Force Survey.

Figure 1.9 Underemployment Rates, by Job Type

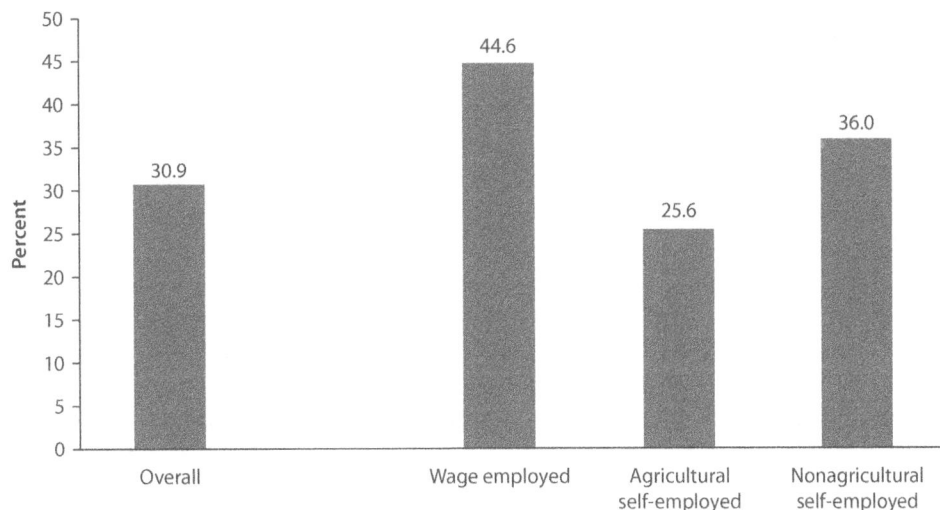

Source: 2014 Sierra Leone Labor Force Survey.

self-employed. Furthermore, 72.9 percent of agricultural self-employment occurs in rural areas, where the underemployment rate is also lowest across all locations.

Earnings

Statistical analysis shows that the determinants of individual earnings resemble those in other countries in the developing world.[13] Holding other characteristics constant, the results show that men earn nearly three times as much as women in wage employment, more than 2.5 times as much in nonagricultural self-employment, and nearly double in agricultural self-employment. The earning gap between individuals with technical degrees or certificates or with tertiary degrees and individuals with less education is highly significant in wage employment and agricultural self-employment; even graduates of upper-secondary school earn 85.0 percent lower wages. Disabled workers earn 13.0 percent less in wage jobs and 45.0 percent less in agricultural self-employment, but 2.7 times more in nonagricultural self-employment. This differential may indicate there is some discrimination among wage employers against disabled workers and workers adapting to market conditions. Because disabled workers earn less in wage jobs at any given level of education, more productive disabled workers (along dimensions other than schooling) may be opting for self-employment, whereas more productive nondisabled workers may be choosing wage employment.

Mining, Freetown and, to a lesser extent, other urban areas, and private sector wage jobs provide the highest earnings. Even NGOs and international organizations pay an average of 7 percent less for a comparable worker, and wages are 18 percent lower among wage employees in the public sector than in the private sector. Mining offers the highest paying jobs in nonagricultural self-employment and the second highest paying jobs in wage employment (behind construction).

Findings from the 2014 Labor Force Survey in Sierra Leone
http://dx.doi.org/10.1596/978-1-4648-0742-8

Wage employment in agriculture pays the least, whereas, among the nonagricultural self-employed, construction pays the least. These results suggest that wage employment in construction may be quite selective, and the nonagricultural self-employed in the construction sector are likely doing particularly low-productivity work.

There is significant variation in income poverty rates across districts (map 1.5). Combining all income sources captured in the Sierra Leone Labor Force Survey (SLLFS) (wage income, household enterprise profits, and agricultural income) for all household members, one can construct an income poverty measure at the household level.[14] Although this measure excludes income from other sources (financial income, rental income, remittances, transfers), it potentially captures all the sources of labor-generated income available to the household. Income poverty differs from consumption poverty in key dimensions, and thus comparison of income poverty measures and consumption poverty measures, such as those reported in the Sierra Leone Poverty Assessment (2013), should be interpreted with care.[15] Keeping these caveats in mind and following the international standard of $2.00 per consumption unit per day, the results show that poverty rates vary from a low of 18.3 percent in Koinadugu and 19.6 percent in Kambia to a high of 83.7 percent in Moyamba, 76.0 percent in Bombali, and 72.8 percent in the Western Area Rural District.

The most important contributor to district-level income poverty is lack of work. Employment is more closely associated with lower poverty rates than

Map 1.5   Poverty Rates, $2.00-a-Day Criterion, by District

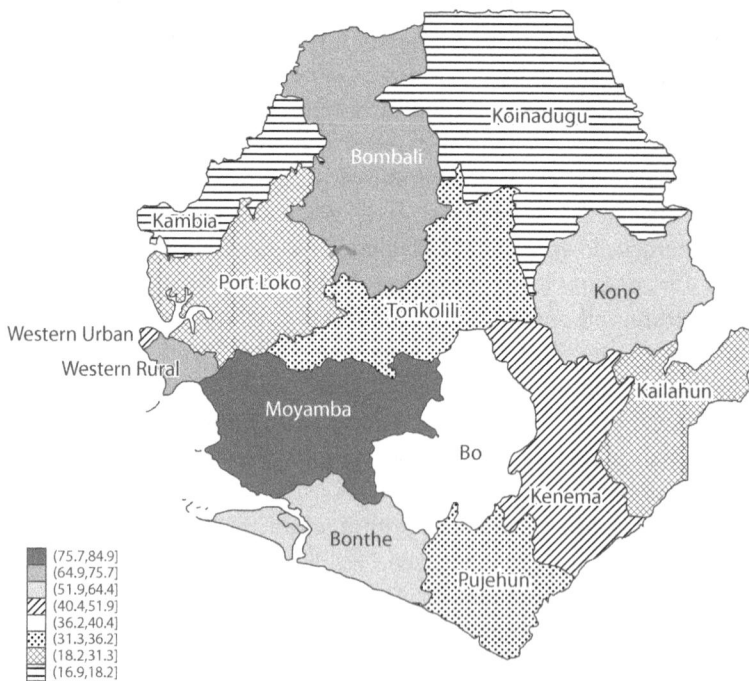

(75.7,84.9]
(64.9,75.7]
(51.9,64.4]
(40.4,51.9]
(36.2,40.4]
(31.3,36.2]
(18.2,31.3]
(16.9,18.2]

Source: 2014 Sierra Leone Labor Force Survey.

skills, job type, sector of activity, or even earnings while employed (figure 1.10). Because poverty is a household-level phenomenon, each additional person in a household who is working relative to a given household size reduces the risk that the household will be poor. Although some types of jobs pay more than others, the difference in household income that is generated by a household member changing jobs is typically less than the gain if an inactive household member takes up work in a job typical for the district in which the household is located. A similar analysis is valid for education. Although the share of people who have never attended school is highest in rural areas, these areas also have higher employment rates, and the simple fact that more people are working outweighs the negative effect on earnings of illiteracy or limited education. This does not imply that skills can be neglected, for skills improve the productivity of labor, improve the livelihoods of the people with the skills, and push the country toward more development. It does, however, highlight how crucial jobs are to poverty reduction, and enhancing labor force participation and job creation can be effective tools in reducing poverty.

In a similar vein, employment in the agriculture sector does more to reduce poverty than employment in the mining sector, which has been driving the country's GDP growth in recent years. Although jobs in agriculture are not particularly well paid, the sector does more to reduce poverty because it provides more jobs. Thus, although districts with a larger share of mining employment may have some people earning more money, there are so few mining jobs that the associated bump in income is only narrowly distributed, and the correlation with poverty

Figure 1.10 Correlation of District Poverty Rates and Key Labor Market Indicators

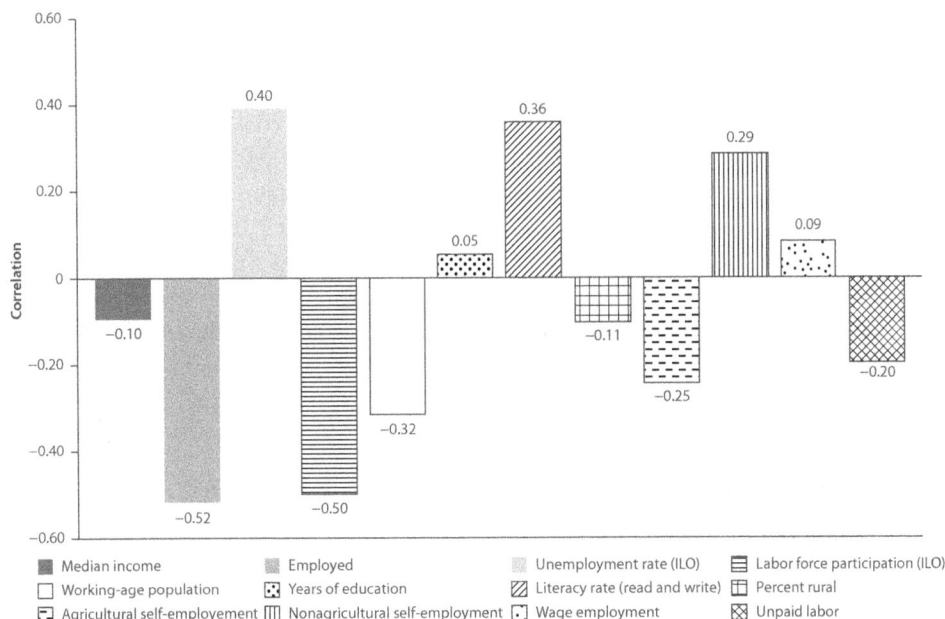

Legend:
- Median income
- Working-age population
- Agricultural self-employment
- Employed
- Years of education
- Nonagricultural self-employment
- Unemployment rate (ILO)
- Literacy rate (read and write)
- Wage employment
- Labor force participation (ILO)
- Percent rural
- Unpaid labor

Source: 2014 Sierra Leone Labor Force Survey.

Findings from the 2014 Labor Force Survey in Sierra Leone
http://dx.doi.org/10.1596/978-1-4648-0742-8

Figure 1.11 Correlation of District Poverty Rates and Sector of Employment

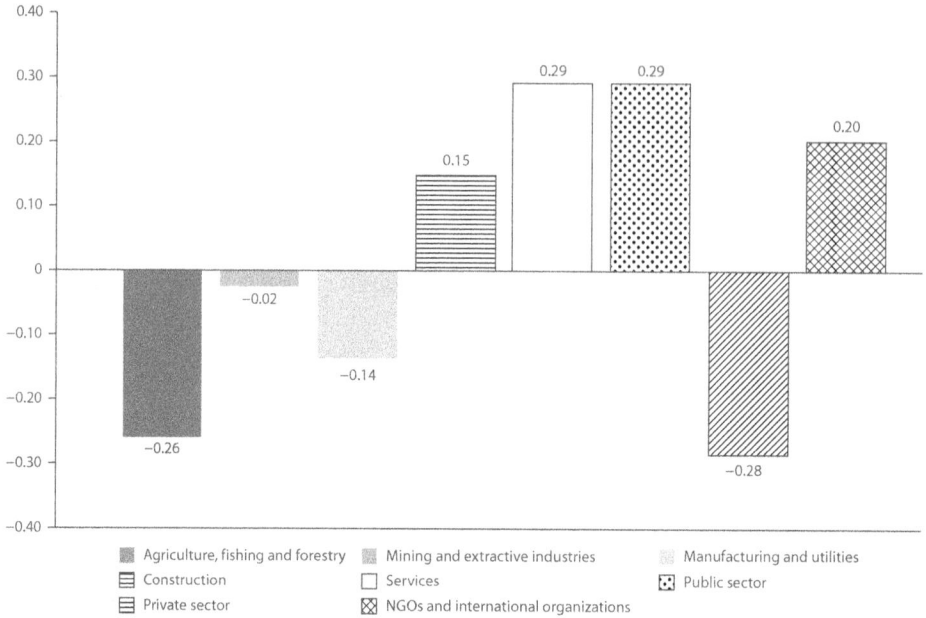

Source: 2014 Sierra Leone Labor Force Survey.

rates is minimal (figure 1.11). In addition, districts with a flourishing private sector have lower poverty rates than districts with relatively large public sectors.

Not only is poverty an issue, but inequality across household incomes is high, and only a small portion of the working-age population has benefited from employment programs. Although the average per consumption unit was Le 1,296,084, the median per consumption unit was only Le 206,277 (figure 1.12). One-quarter of households had a per consumption unit below Le 6,000. At the other end of the spectrum, the top 10 percent of households all had a per consumption unit over Le 1,496,667, and the top 1 percent were all over Le 15,000,000. Few workers benefit from any employment-related social protection programs that can help protect them against income poverty; only 1.8 percent reported that they had directly benefited in the last 12 months from any such programs run by the government, donors, or NGOs. Youth reported that they benefited from the Smallholder Commercialization Program most frequently (36 percent). There are no noticeable differences across gender or place of residence among the respondents who reported they benefited from social protection programs.

Unemployment

Unemployment Rates

The overall unemployment rate masks significant variations in unemployment rates across districts and subpopulations.[16] The overall share of the unemployed in the workforce is 4.3 percent, but unemployment rates vary across districts

Figure 1.12 Distribution of Household Income per Consumption Unit

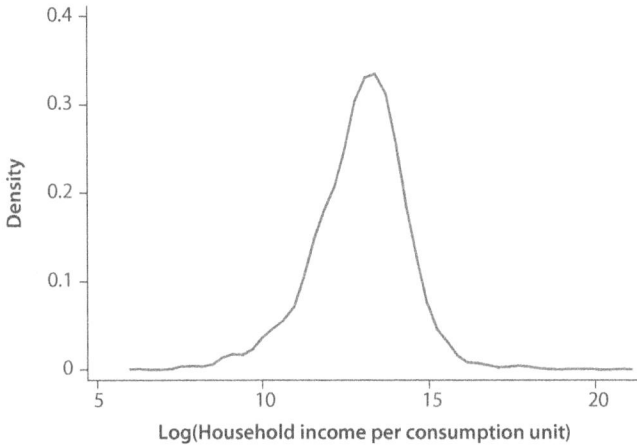

kernel = epanechnikov, bandwidth = 0.2000

Source: 2014 Sierra Leone Labor Force Survey.

Map 1.6 Unemployment Rates (ILO), by District

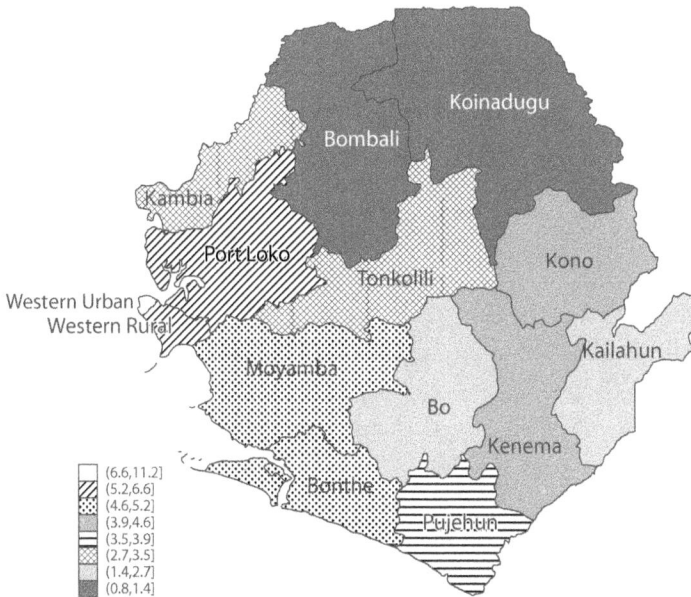

Source: 2014 Sierra Leone Labor Force Survey.

from as low as 0.8 percent in Kailahun to as high as 11.2 percent in the Western Area Urban District (map 1.6). Across types of people, one also finds important variations, especially in comparing urban Freetown, other urban areas, and rural residents, as well as across disability status (Figure 1.13). Taking into account educational attainment, the lowest unemployment rates observed are among people with no education, while the highest unemployment rates are among individuals with technical degrees or certificates (figure 1.14).

Findings from the 2014 Labor Force Survey in Sierra Leone
http://dx.doi.org/10.1596/978-1-4648-0742-8

Figure 1.13   Unemployment Rates (ILO), by Characteristics of Individuals

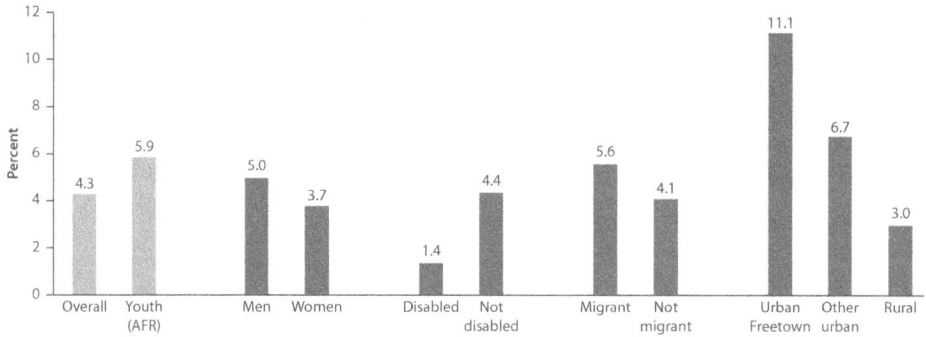

Source: 2014 Sierra Leone Labor Force Survey.

Figure 1.14   Unemployment Rates (ILO), by Educational Attainment and Province

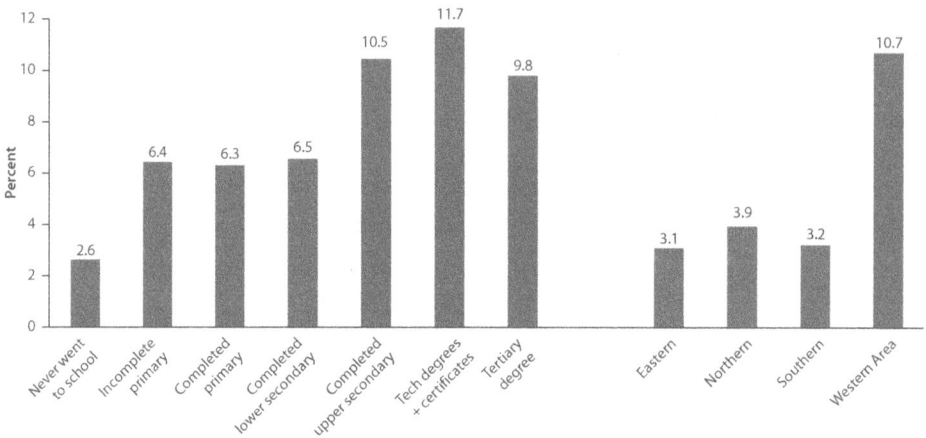

Source: 2014 Sierra Leone Labor Force Survey.

Only 2.8 percent of the working-age population is unemployed according to the ILO definition, while 9.1 percent are included among the broad unemployed.[17] This implies that, among the working-age population, 6.3 percent do not have jobs and are not actively searching for work.[18] There is significant variation across types of people, educational level, and location (figure 1.15). For example, 42.2 percent of migrants who are available for work, but not working are actively searching for work, whereas only 28.8 percent of the broad nonmigrant unemployed are actively searching for work.[19] Likewise, there are relatively few people with tertiary degrees who are among the broad unemployed and who are not looking for work (29.6 percent), whereas a much larger share of those who have never attended school and who are not working, but are available for work, are not actively searching for work (77.4 percent) (figure 1.16). Geographically, individuals living in the Western Area (48.2 percent) and, particularly, in the Western Area Urban District (49.1 percent) are the most likely to be searching for work if they are among the broad unemployed, while only 11.5 percent of the unemployed in Koinadugu District are actively looking for work.

Figure 1.15 Share of Working-Age Population Unemployed, by Characteristics of Individuals

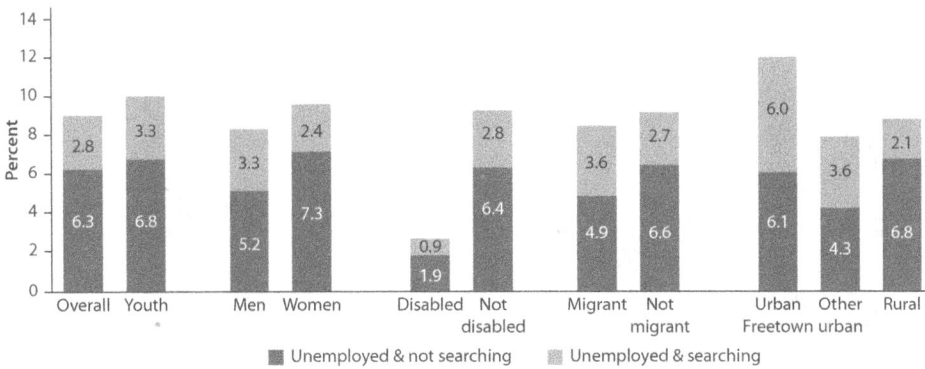

Source: 2014 Sierra Leone Labor Force Survey.

Figure 1.16 Share of Working-Age Population Unemployed, by Educational Attainment and Province

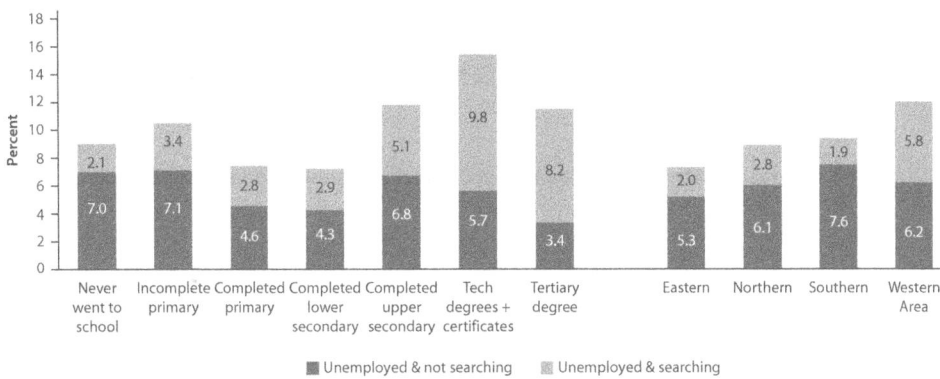

Source: 2014 Sierra Leone Labor Force Survey.

How the Unemployed Search for Work

The unemployed who are actively looking for work mostly rely on family and friendship ties to find jobs (figure 1.17). Among the unemployed, 52.8 percent seek the assistance of their friends and relatives to find work. Women rely more than men on the assistance of friends and relatives to find work (64.3 percent vs. 42.2 percent). Community ties tend to be more tightly knit in rural areas than in urban areas, which explains the importance of the assistance of friends and relatives in looking for work in rural areas relative to urban areas (61.4 percent vs. 43.1 percent). The second most important strategy is to check at current workplaces or other worksites, farms, factory gates, markets (altogether, 24.3 percent); this strategy is used more heavily by men than by women (32.8 percent vs. 14.9 percent), though it is much less frequent in urban Freetown. To find work, the disabled register at public or private employment exchanges much more often than other groups.

The unemployed at lower levels of education rely more frequently than the unemployed at higher levels of education on the assistance of friends and relatives to find work (figure 1.18). Unemployed individuals who have never

Findings from the 2014 Labor Force Survey in Sierra Leone
http://dx.doi.org/10.1596/978-1-4648-0742-8

Figure 1.17 Job Search Strategies among the Unemployed, by Educational Attainment and Location

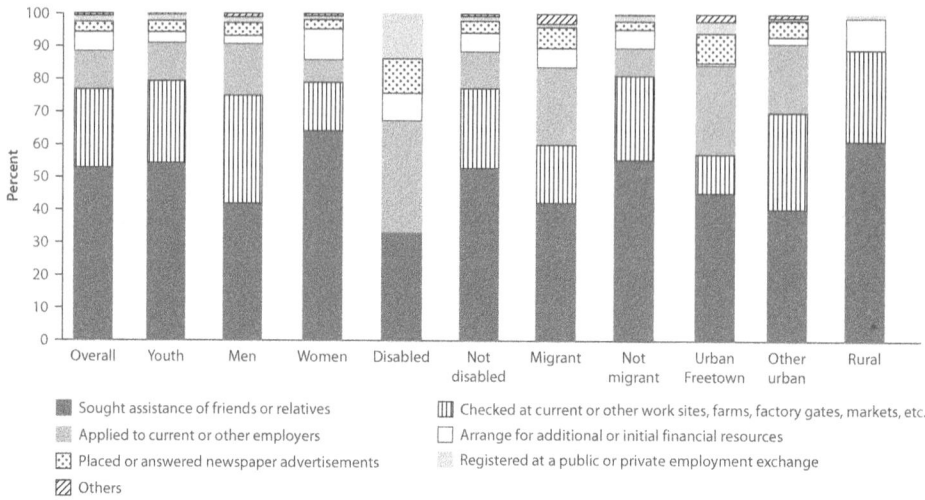

Sought assistance of friends or relatives

Applied to current or other employers

Placed or answered newspaper advertisements

Others

Checked at current or other work sites, farms, factory gates, markets, etc.

Arrange for additional or initial financial resources

Registered at a public or private employment exchange

Source: 2014 Sierra Leone Labor Force Survey.
Note: Others includes applying for a permit or looking for land, a building, machinery, or equipment to establish or improve an enterprise.

Figure 1.18 Job Search Strategies among the Unemployed, by Educational Attainment and Province

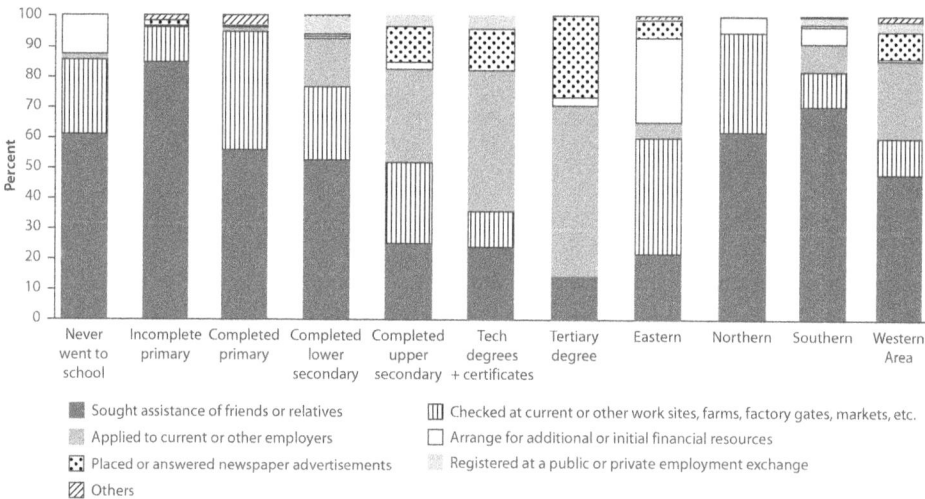

Sought assistance of friends or relatives

Applied to current or other employers

Placed or answered newspaper advertisements

Others

Checked at current or other work sites, farms, factory gates, markets, etc.

Arrange for additional or initial financial resources

Registered at a public or private employment exchange

Source: 2014 Sierra Leone Labor Force Survey.
Note: Others includes applying for a permit or looking for land, a building, machinery, or equipment to establish or improve an enterprise.

attended school use this strategy 61.0 percent of the time, compared with 14.7 percent among the unemployed with tertiary degrees. Seeking the assistance of friends or relatives to find work is the most frequent strategy in Southern Province (70 percent), but it is not as common in Eastern Province (21.8 percent). Applying to current employers or other employers becomes a more important strategy as the level of educational attainment rises.

Reasons Not to Search for Work

The low shares of the unemployed engaging in active searches for work do not reflect laziness, but extenuating circumstances such as a lack of capital, lack of skills, or perceived lack of available jobs. More than half the broad unemployed who are not searching for work report that the reason is their lack of the financial or other resources needed to start a business (figure 1.19).[20] This is followed in importance by those who report they are still in school or in training programs.[21] The next two most common reasons for not searching for work are lack of skills (10.1 percent) and discouragement (7.7 percent), that is, a perceived lack of available jobs. Only 0.5 percent of the broad unemployed reported they were not searching for work because they did not want to work.

The reasons for not searching vary widely across population groups. Women, rural residents, and the disabled are disproportionately affected by capital constraints; migrants and urban Freetown residents are disproportionately discouraged; and men and the disabled are disproportionately likely to be skills constrained. Capital constraints are, by far, the most important reason cited for not searching among individuals who have never attended school (figure 1.20). Among individuals with tertiary degrees, 15.6 percent report they are not searching for work because they are in school or in training programs. Capital constraints are not an issue among people with a tertiary education, although a perceived lack of demand (31.7 percent of responses) is a major problem, and many of these people (23.5 percent) report they are not searching for work because they are waiting for replies to earlier job enquiries.

Capital constraints are particularly binding in Eastern Province, while the reasons for not searching in the Western Area mirror those of urban residents more generally. In Kenema and Kono, 89 percent and 94 percent, respectively, of

Figure 1.19 Reasons for Not Searching for Work, by Characteristics of Unemployed Individuals

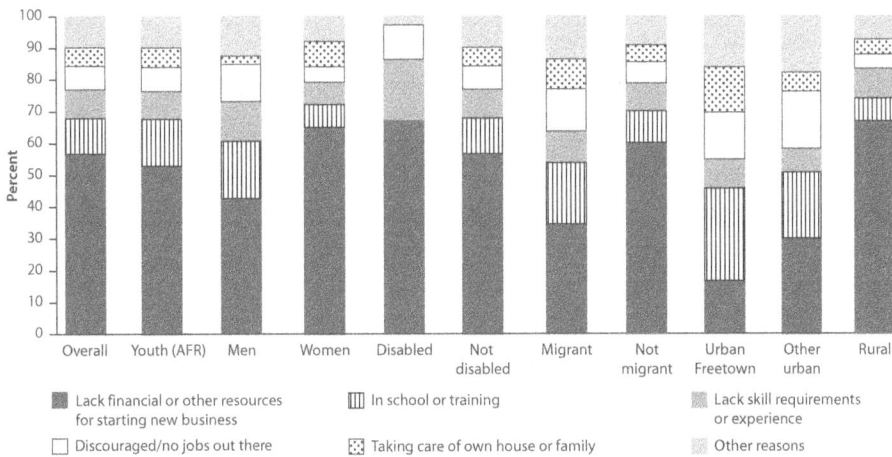

Legend:
- Lack financial or other resources for starting new business
- In school or training
- Lack skill requirements or experience
- Discouraged/no jobs out there
- Taking care of own house or family
- Other reasons

Source: 2014 Sierra Leone Labor Force Survey.
Note: Other reasons include illness or injury, pregnancy, retirement or young age, transportation problems, awaiting replies to earlier inquiries, waiting to start a new job or business, off-season, does not want to work, and so on.

Figure 1.20   Reasons for Not Searching for Work, by Educational Attainment and Province

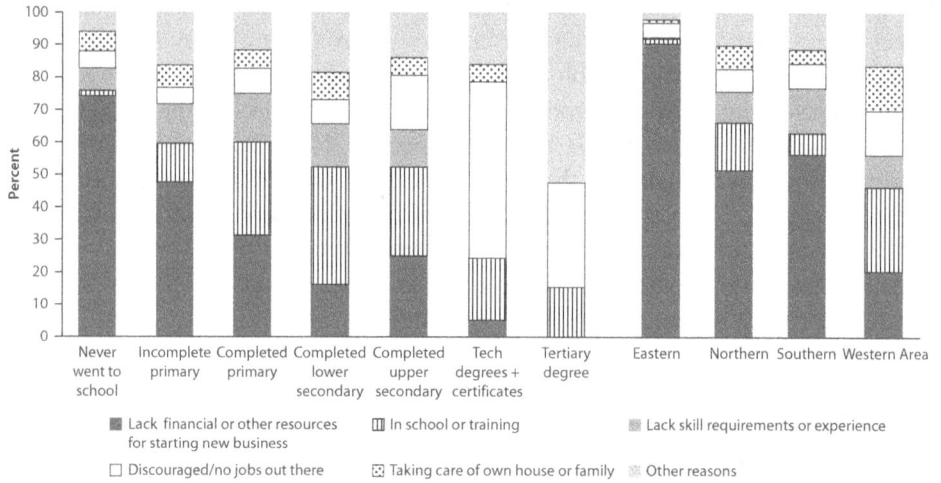

Source: 2014 Sierra Leone Labor Force Survey.
Note: Other reasons include illness or injury, pregnancy, retirement or young age, transportation problems, awaiting replies to earlier inquiries, waiting to start a new job or business, off-season, does not want to work, and so on.

the broad unemployed who are not looking for work report they are not searching because of capital constraints; the second most common reason is discouragement, but this only affects 6.7 percent of the broad unemployed in Kenema, and 1.3 percent in Kono. In the Western Area Urban District, capital constraints are only relevant among 16.0 percent of the broad unemployed, whereas 28.0 percent are still in school.

Migration

Younger cohorts include fewer migrants, and the effects of war on internal migration have largely dissipated. Figure 1.21 shows that international migration is a minor phenomenon; the share of international migrants has not recently exceeded 8 percent of all migrants. The share of migrants is relatively stable at around 18 percent of any given age cohort from the late 20s age group on, although there is a small peak in the 47–54 age group, where up to a quarter of the age group is represented by internal migrants. Given that the SLLFS took place in 2014, this small peak corresponds to people who were in the 24–31 age group at the start of the war.

The reasons for migration change with age, shifting from an orientation toward education to work, although marriage remains the most important except among the youngest age groups. Among the youngest age groups, school and training are as dominant as marriage or maintenance of family and friendships among the factors behind migration, each representing roughly 40 percent of the reported reasons (figure 1.22). As people age, school becomes a less important factor, while migration for work becomes increasingly important. Conflict-related reasons are key among migrants in their early 30s, as well as among older age groups.[22]

Figure 1.21 Internal and International Migration

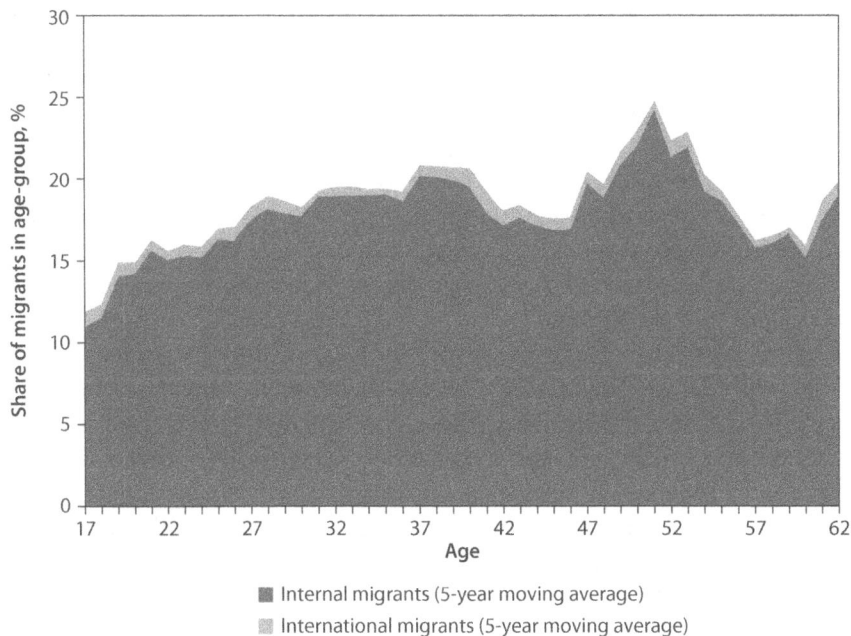

Internal migrants (5-year moving average)
International migrants (5-year moving average)

Source: 2014 Sierra Leone Labor Force Survey.

Figure 1.22 Reasons for Migration, by Age (Five-Year Moving Average)

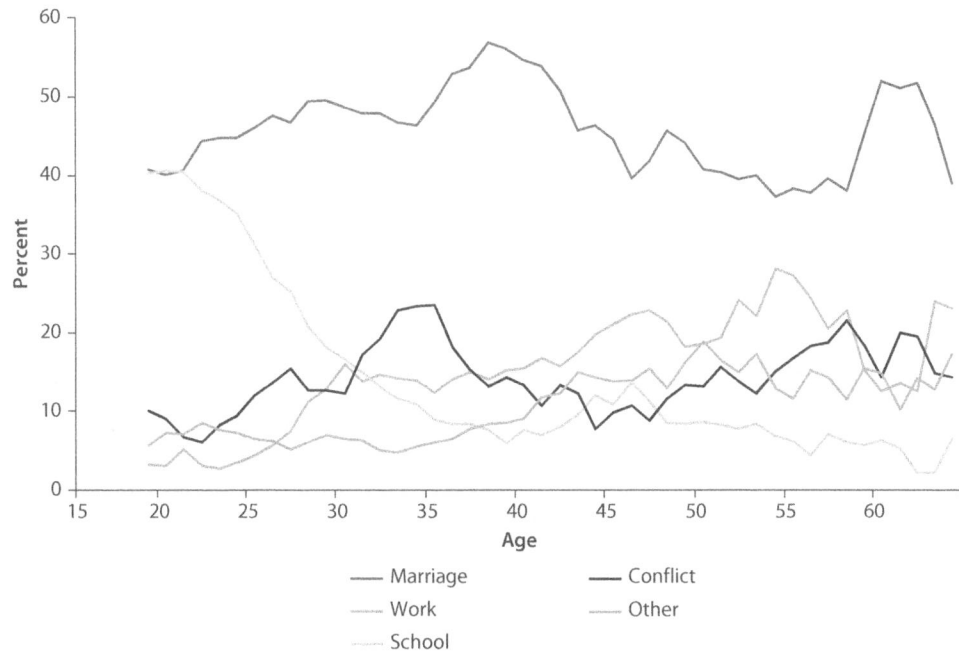

Marriage   Conflict
Work   Other
School

Source: 2014 Sierra Leone Labor Force Survey.

Findings from the 2014 Labor Force Survey in Sierra Leone
http://dx.doi.org/10.1596/978-1-4648-0742-8

Although difficult to disentangle from age effects, the civil conflict clearly influenced migration behavior. The share of people who migrated because of a threat of physical violence was 1.5 percentage points higher among people who were of school age during the conflict relative to people who entered school after the conflict and 1.8 percentage points higher relative to people who reached working age before the conflict began (figure 1.23). However, this older group was 2.7 percentage points more likely to have migrated because their property had been destroyed or occupied during the war relative to people who were of school age during the war (and who were thus less likely to have owned property during the war) and 3.1 percentage points higher relative to people who started school after the war had ended.

The motivation for migration varies with the level of education. At 64 percent, the least well-educated migrants are the most likely to have migrated to marry (figure 1.24). The importance of marriage as a motive for migration declines with educational attainment, whereas migration to attend school or for training increases and is the main motivation among migrants with at least upper-secondary education. Migration for work is prevalent among migrants with postsecondary educational attainment and, after migration for work, is the second most frequently cited reason for migration among this group. Conflict is also an important motive for migration.

Statistical analysis of the reasons for migration shows results similar to those above.[23] The average man is 3.15 percentage points less likely to migrate to marry than the average woman. People with less than a postsecondary education, espe-

Figure 1.23 Reasons for Migration, by Age Group during the Conflict

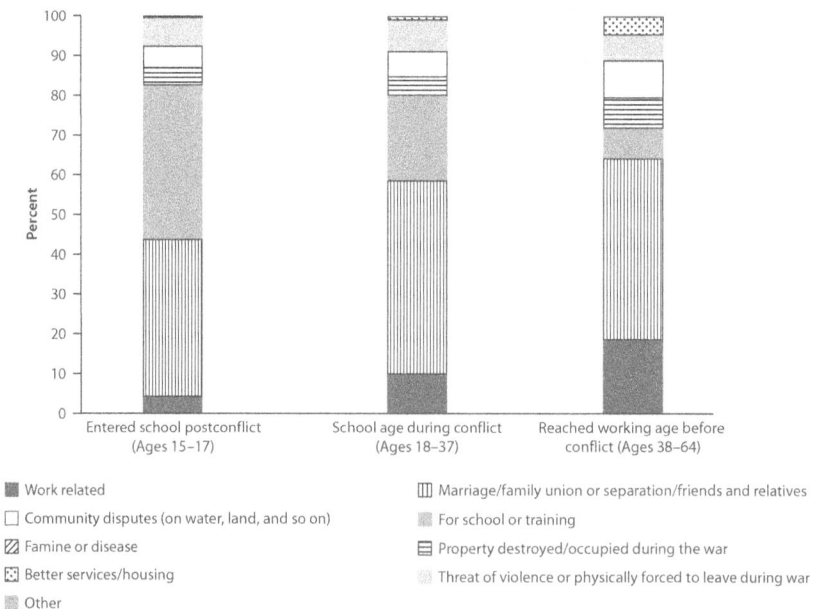

Work related

Community disputes (on water, land, and so on)

Famine or disease

Better services/housing

Other

Marriage/family union or separation/friends and relatives

For school or training

Property destroyed/occupied during the war

Threat of violence or physically forced to leave during war

Source: 2014 Sierra Leone Labor Force Survey.

Findings from the 2014 Labor Force Survey in Sierra Leone
http://dx.doi.org/10.1596/978-1-4648-0742-8

Figure 1.24 Reasons for Migration, by Educational Attainment

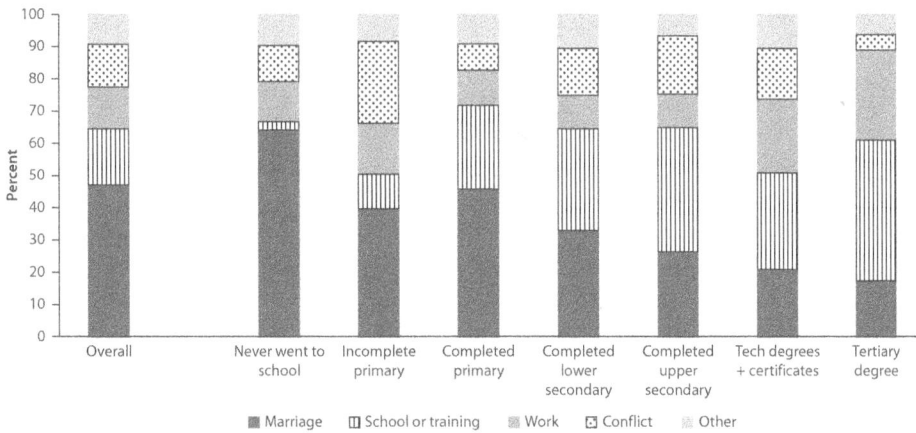

Source: 2014 Sierra Leone Labor Force Survey.

cially those who have never attended school, are also less likely to migrate to marry. Individuals of prime working age (35–50) and urban residents, especially residents of Freetown, are significantly more likely to migrate to marry. People who migrate for school and people who migrate for work are similar in characteristics. They are typically young men (less than 20 years of age) with postsecondary degrees who are living in urban areas, especially Freetown.

Notes

1. Disability status is self-declared and includes the following situations: limited use of legs, loss of leg(s), limited use of arms, loss of arm(s), problems with back or spine, hearing difficulty, deaf (no hearing), sight difficulty, blind, speech impairment, mute (nonspeaking), mental retardation, mental illness, and other. Migrants are defined as individuals residing in districts that are not the districts in which they were born.

2. An important caveat affecting this report is that the sample has been designed to be representative of district populations, but not along any particular decomposition of the workforce. This implies that the statistics presented here are subject to more sampling error when considering subpopulations on which there are few observations (for example, the disabled or individuals with higher-education degrees); thus, the interpretation of the results should not be generalized to the population as a whole.

3. The working-age population is defined as individuals between 15 and 64 years of age.

4. The labor force is defined as the sum of those people who are employed and those who are unemployed.

5. The results on people with technical degrees and certificates, and tertiary degrees should be treated with caution, as they are calculated based on 70 and 19 observations, respectively.

6. The employment-to-population ratio is equal to the total employed, divided by the working-age population.

Findings from the 2014 Labor Force Survey in Sierra Leone
http://dx.doi.org/10.1596/978-1-4648-0742-8

7. Members of producer cooperatives, a separate category of employment designated by the ILO, are included here under agricultural self-employment.

8. According to Gindling and Newhouse (2012), the average share of wage and salary workers, which can include agricultural wage labor, was 13.4 percent in Sub-Saharan African countries. Among the employed, 63.7 percent were in agriculture, and 20.4 percent were in self-employment (plus 2.4 percent in unpaid work).

9. A multinomial logit model has been estimated by type of job. The results can be found in appendix B, table B.13.

10. The potential for the mining sector to generate employment in other sectors indirectly, in particular as a client for household enterprises involved in services, is limited. Household enterprises tend to be largely engaged in petty trade (see chapter 3), and additional analysis finds that only 5 percent of household enterprises sell to the mining sector.

11. The category includes the national government, local governments, public or state-owned enterprises, and parastatal entities.

12. The underemployment rate is the percentage of individuals who desire to work more among all those who are working an average of less than 8 hours a day.

13. The regression analysis consists of a selection bias–corrected wage regression. See appendix B for details.

14. The SLLFS provides information on income from agricultural activities, but not on expenditures. Thus, constructing a profits measure for agricultural activities is impossible. This implies an overestimation of total net household income and an underestimation of income poverty rates relative to what would have been found had expenditures also been measured. Meanwhile, to calculate an income poverty measure, one needs to divide household income by the number of consumption units in the household. We have used an equivalence scale that counts each adult as 1 and each child as 0.5 to calculate the number of household consumption units.

15. For example, production for household consumption is valued using a consumption poverty measure, whereas an income poverty measure would exclude this production. Also, durable goods can provide consumption value for years after their purchase, while an income poverty measure would only capture the resources used to purchase the durable goods in the year in which they were purchased.

16. The unemployment rate (4.3 percent) refers to the total unemployed divided by the total workforce (working-age population unemployed plus employed, excluding those who do not participate in the labor market). In table 1.1, the 2.8 percent refers to the share of unemployed (that is, total unemployed divided by the total working-age population).

17. See the previous footnote for clarification.

18. The 6.3 percent is a result of subtracting the ILO unemployed (2.8 percent) from the broad unemployed (9.1 percent). What is left represents those people who do not have jobs and who are not looking for work.

19. The rate of those actively searching for work among the broad unemployed is obtained by dividing the unemployment rate according to the ILO definition by the rate of the broad unemployed. This contrasts with the share of the unemployed who are not actively searching for work.

20. Only 69.6 percent of the broad unemployed provided a reason for not searching, which introduces the possibility of selection bias in the results. Thus, among groups

defined by educational attainment, those more likely to respond are also more likely to report they are capital constrained and less likely to be discouraged. This implies that, if those who do respond are typical of their subgroups, the results presented here may overestimate the importance of capital constraints and underestimate the importance of discouragement.

21. In principle, individuals still in school should not consider themselves available to start work. The data thus suggest there is a weak attachment to the educational system that merits further analysis.

22. Conflict-related reasons include property destroyed or occupied during the war, the threat of violence, physical threats, and community disputes over water, land, and so on.

23. This analysis is based on a multinomial logit model of the motives for migration. See appendix B.

CHAPTER 2

Skills

This chapter discusses the skills available in the labor force along three dimensions: educational attainment, training, and apprenticeships. It first presents a detailed analysis of literacy, followed by a discussion of educational attainment, education providers, and the reasons for ending the school experience. After the overview of formal education, it presents an analysis of training and apprenticeships. It closes with an examination of the links between skills and earnings (photo 2.1).

Literacy

Literacy rates among the working-age population are low, and there are noticeable differences across subgroups.[1] More than half the working-age population (56.7 percent) and almost all (96.9 percent) of those individuals who have never attended school can neither read nor write, which classifies them as illiterate (figure 2.1). The illiteracy rate is higher among women than among men (66.4 percent vs. 45.1 percent) and higher among the disabled than among the nondisabled (72.3 percent vs. 56.3 percent). A larger share of the rural population is illiterate (68.0 percent); this compares with urban Freetown (20.4 percent) and other urban areas (34.1 percent), which partly reflects the greater access to education in urban areas.

Literacy rates among the working population across the country largely mirror the urban–rural distribution. Northern Province has the highest rate of illiteracy (66.1 percent), followed by Eastern Province (61.5 percent), Southern Province (55.6 percent), and, at a much lower illiteracy rate, the Western Area (22.6 percent) (map 2.1). As suggested in the migration discussion (chapter 1), educational opportunities are more abundant in urban areas, leaving rural residents with relatively less access to even the basic level of education needed to read and write.

Photo 2.1   Students listening closely at a vocational training center in Bo

Photo Credit: Andrea Martin.

Figure 2.1   Literacy Rates among the Working-Age Population, by Characteristics of Individuals

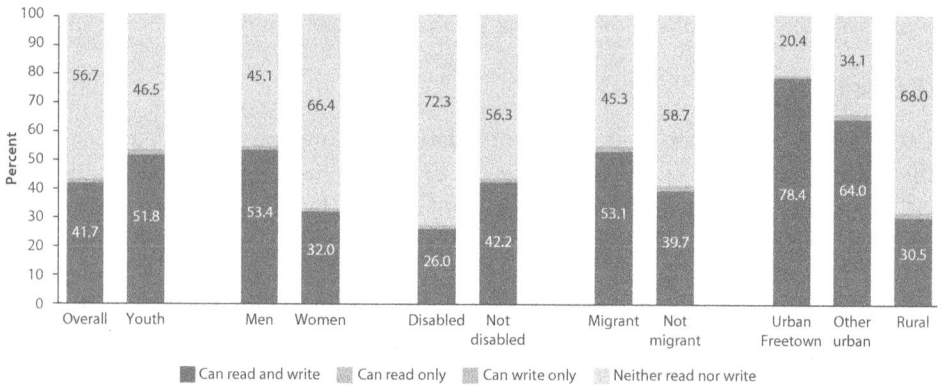

■ Can read and write   ▨ Can read only   ▨ Can write only   ▨ Neither read nor write

Source: 2014 Sierra Leone Labor Force Survey.

Educational Attainment

Overall, more than half the working-age population has never attended school, and attendance rates vary widely across subgroups (figure 2.2). The proportion of those who have never attended school is greater among women than men (63.7 percent vs. 44.9 percent). Disabled individuals seem to have less access to formal education than the nondisabled because 70.9 percent of the disabled have never attended school. Migrants show greater average educational attainment than nonmigrants, which reflects, among other factors, that most migrants live in urban areas, where educational attainment is greater, and that acquiring more education is frequently the primary reason for migration (see chapter 1).

Map 2.1   Literacy Rates (Read and Write), by District

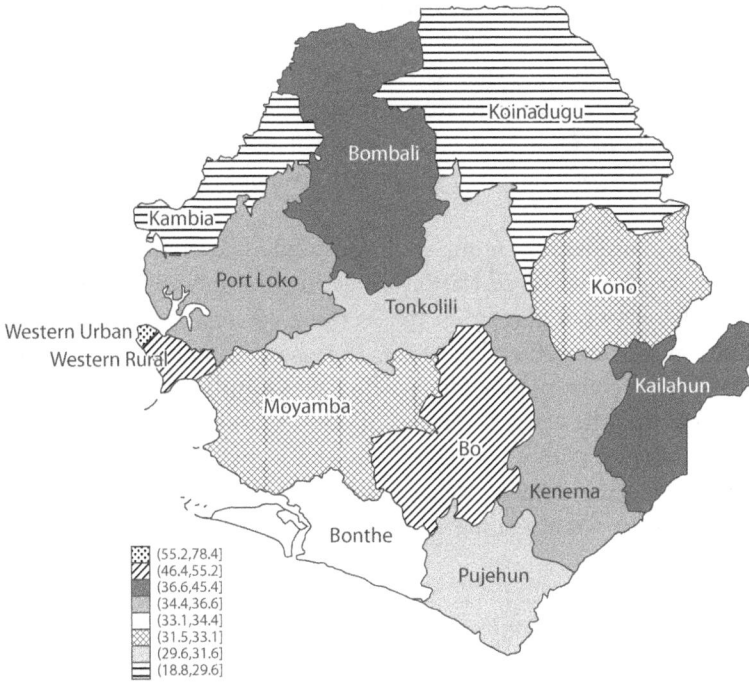

Legend:
[55.2,78.4]
[46.4,55.2]
[36.6,45.4]
[34.4,36.6]
[33.1,34.4]
[31.5,33.1]
[29.6,31.6]
[18.8,29.6]

Source: 2014 Sierra Leone Labor Force Survey.

Figure 2.2   Educational Attainment, by Characteristics of Working-Age Individuals

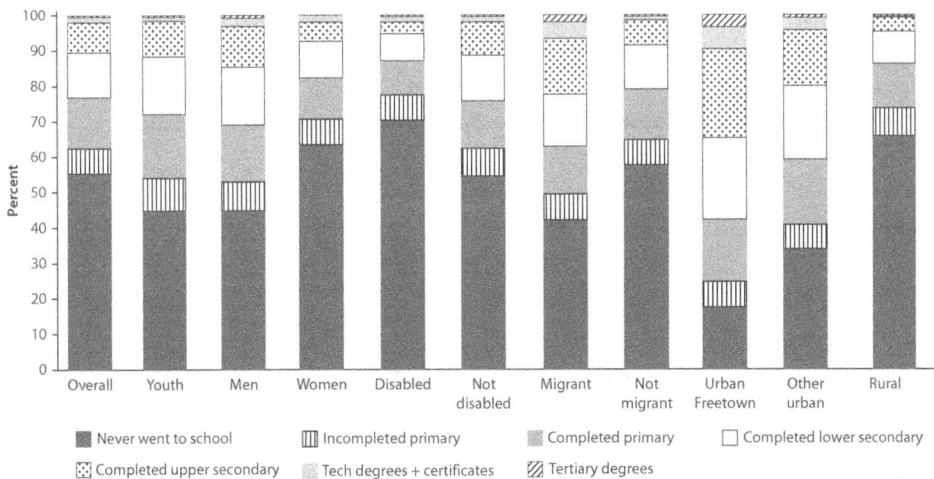

Legend:
■ Never went to school   ▥ Incompleted primary   ▨ Completed primary   □ Completed lower secondary
▦ Completed upper secondary   ▤ Tech degrees + certificates   ▧ Tertiary degrees

Source: 2014 Sierra Leone Labor Force Survey.

Findings from the 2014 Labor Force Survey in Sierra Leone
http://dx.doi.org/10.1596/978-1-4648-0742-8

Almost 8 in 10 individuals in the working-age population have attained, at most, primary education, while only a small fraction of the population has attained higher educational levels. For example, less than 1 percent of the working-age population has tertiary degrees. There are clear gender disparities in educational attainment: a greater percentage of men than women complete primary school or lower- or upper-secondary school. Urban residents also have completed higher levels of education in greater proportion relative to rural inhabitants.

Urban areas are considerably more well educated than rural areas, likely driven by greater availability of education infrastructure and ability to afford schooling. In rural areas, 66.4 percent of the working-age population has never attended school, while, in urban Freetown, the share is only 17.5 percent (figure 2.3). In urban Freetown, individuals who have completed upper-secondary school make up the largest share of the working-age population (25.3 percent), compared with 15.7 percent in other urban areas and only 3.8 percent in rural areas. See section "Reasons for Not Attending School" for a discussion of reasons for not attending school and differences across urban and rural areas.

Reasons for Not Attending School

Among the working-age population, the main reason for never attending school is financial constraints (42.2 percent) (figure 2.4). Other commonly cited reasons include the decision of families not to allow schooling (32.0 percent) and lack of trust in the value of education (16.5 percent). Family decisions not to allow schooling, as well as the lack of trust in the value of education, represent a greater barrier among women than among men. In urban Freetown, the greatest barrier to education is the decision of families not to allow schooling

Figure 2.3 Educational Attainment among the Working-Age Population, by Location

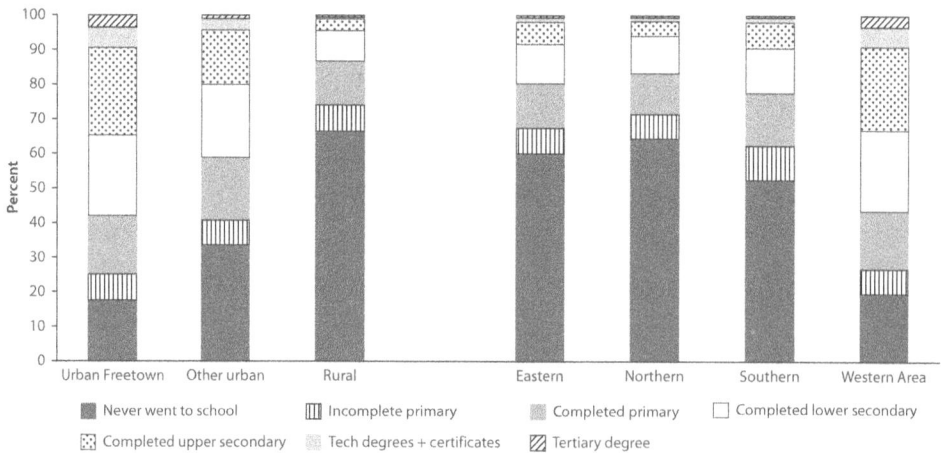

Source: 2014 Sierra Leone Labor Force Survey.

Figure 2.4 The Reasons for Never Attending School, by Characteristics of Individuals

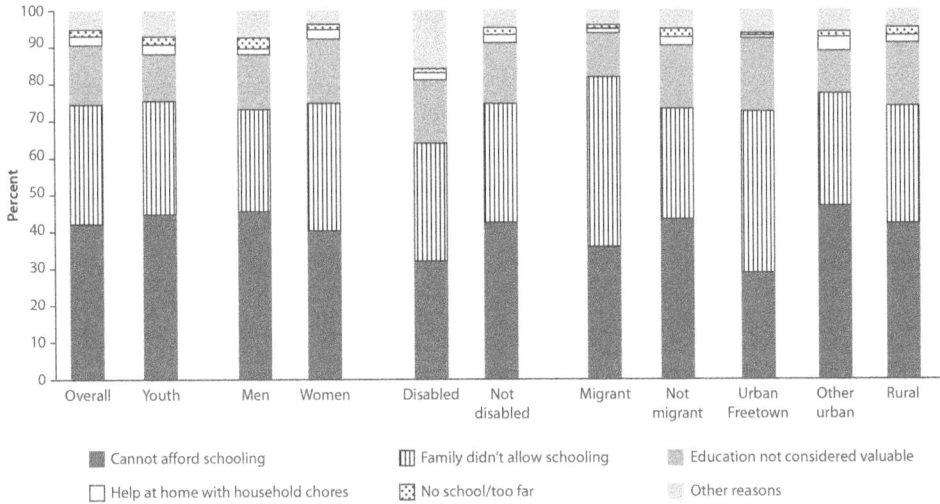

Source: 2014 Sierra Leone Labor Force Survey.

(43.6 percent). The corresponding shares are smaller in other urban areas (30.1 percent) and in rural areas (31.8 percent). In urban areas other than urban Freetown, the greatest barrier to attendance is the cost of schooling (47.0 percent). The corresponding shares are smaller in urban Freetown (28.9 percent) and in rural areas (42.1 percent).

Years of Schooling

Across dimensions such as place of residence and migration status, the average years of education of working-age individuals can vary by more than a year (figures 2.5 and 2.6).[2] The most striking difference in average years of education is between urban and rural areas. Working-age individuals in urban Freetown have an average of 2.4 more years of education than rural residents (10.2 years vs. 7.8 years). There are also gender differences, though they are not as large. Thus, working-age women have around 0.6 fewer years of education than working-age men.

Migrants are at an advantage in years of education; they have an average of 9.8 years of education compared with the 8.5 years of nonmigrants. This derives from several factors. First, 67.0 percent of all migrants live in urban areas, where average years of education are greater than in rural areas. Second, migration is often undertaken with the explicit purpose of acquiring more education (see chapter 1). Third, migrants are less likely to work in low-skilled sectors such agriculture and more likely to work in the more highly skilled service sector.

Geographically, skill composition varies across locations, but the clear leader in average years of education is the Western Area, at 10.2 average years of education. It is followed by Eastern Province (8.4 years), Southern Province (8.3 years), and Northern Province (8.2 years), all about two fewer average

Figure 2.5 Average Years of Schooling, by Characteristics of Individuals in the Working-Age Population

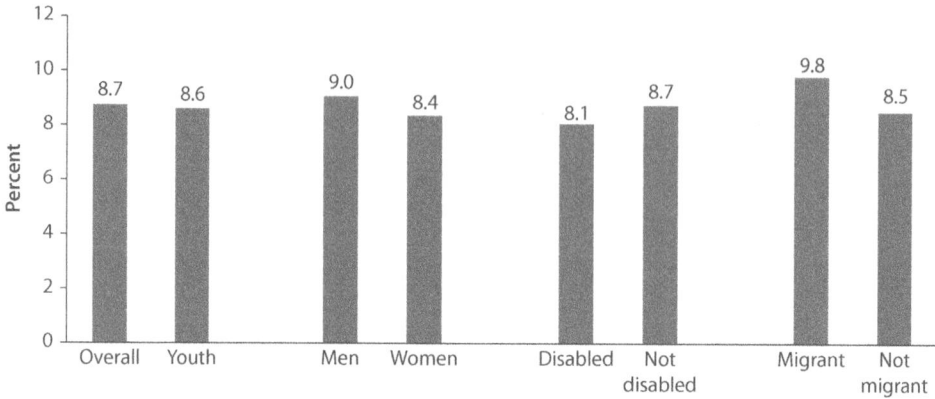

Source: 2014 Sierra Leone Labor Force Survey.

Figure 2.6 Average Years of Education, by Urban or Rural Area and Province

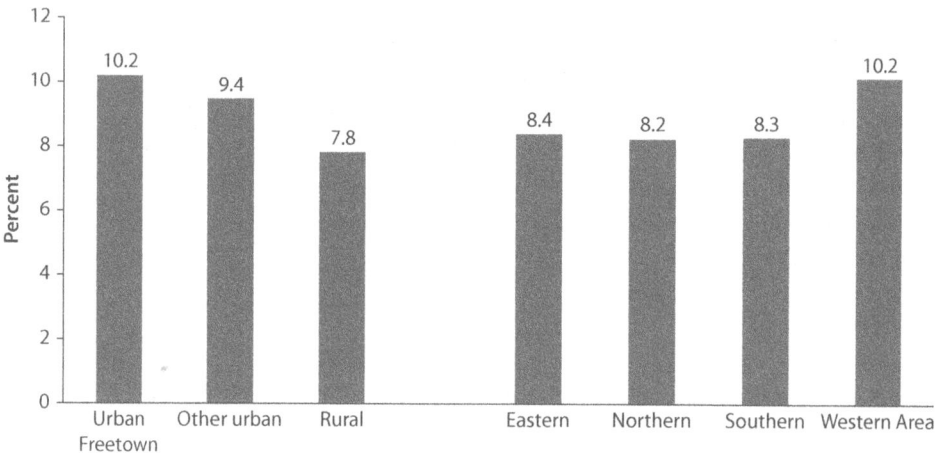

Source: 2014 Sierra Leone Labor Force Survey.

years of education. The variation in average years of education across districts is large (figure 2.6). The most well-educated district has more than three additional years of education, on average, than the least well-educated district. The districts with the most well-educated working-age population are the Western Area Urban District (10.2 years), the Western Area Rural District (9.6 years), and Bo District (9.0 years). The districts with the least well-educated working-age population are Pujehun (7.1 years), Bonthe (7.3 years), and Moyamba (7.5 years).

Education Providers

The vast majority (81.0 percent) of the working-age population was educated at public institutions.[3] The presence of other institutions is relatively limited: 16.1 percent were educated at religious institutions, and only 2.9 percent at private institutions. Because public institutions have the main responsibility of

Figure 2.7 Providers of Education, by Characteristics of Individuals

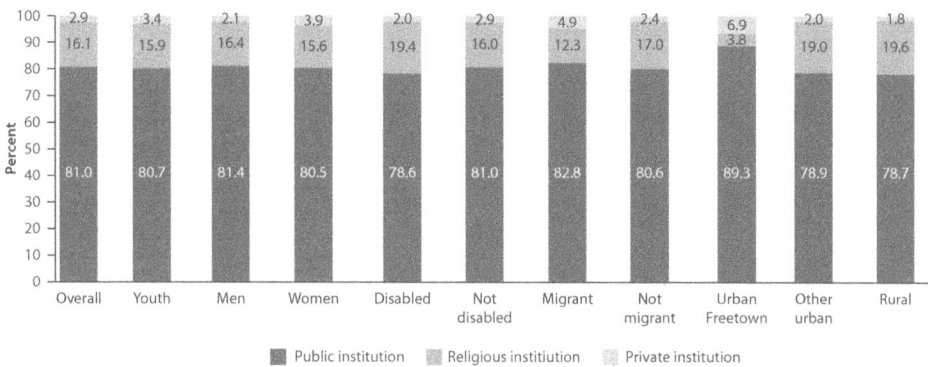

| | Public institution | Religious institution | Private institution |

Source: 2014 Sierra Leone Labor Force Survey.

educating the population, the quality of these institutions is crucial. The relative importance of public institutions is lower in rural areas than in urban areas, while the importance of religious institutions is relatively larger. This may suggest that, in rural areas more than in urban Freetown, religious institutions cover parts of the population that public institutions are not able to reach (figure 2.7). Private educational institutions are not a major supplier of education among any population group, although they educate 6.9 percent of the working-age population in urban Freetown. This is consistent with the fact that residents of urban Freetown enjoy higher incomes than residents in other areas. In other urban and rural areas, only 2.0 percent of the population has attended private institutions.

Training

Only 5.5 percent of the working-age population has participated in vocational training. Considerably more men than women undertake vocational training (7.1 percent vs. 4.2 percent). More people undergo vocational training in urban Freetown (12.6 percent) than in other urban areas (10.0 percent) or in rural areas (3.3 percent). Migrants are also considerably more likely than nonmigrants to obtain vocational training (11.2 percent vs. 4.5 percent).

Most training is undertaken by people who either have never attended school or have started secondary school (figure 2.8). Among the people who have received vocational training, nearly a quarter have never participated in the formal school system, while over 60 percent started secondary school before enrolling in training. Individuals who started primary school but never went on to secondary school comprise less than 15 percent of the people who have enrolled in training courses.

Length of Training

Among individuals in the working-age population who have ever obtained any vocational training, the average duration of training is 2.2 years.[4] The variation

Figure 2.8   Educational Attainment before the Start of Training

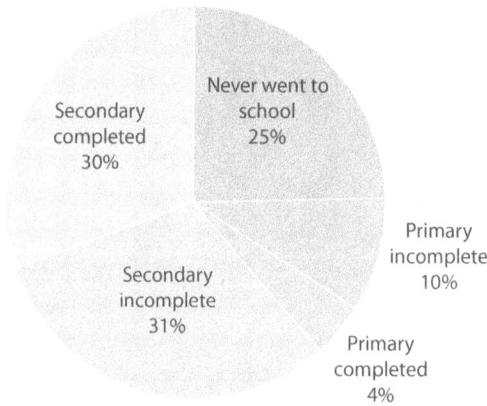

Source: 2014 Sierra Leone Labor Force Survey.

Figure 2.9   Average Years of Training among Trainees, by Characteristics of Individuals

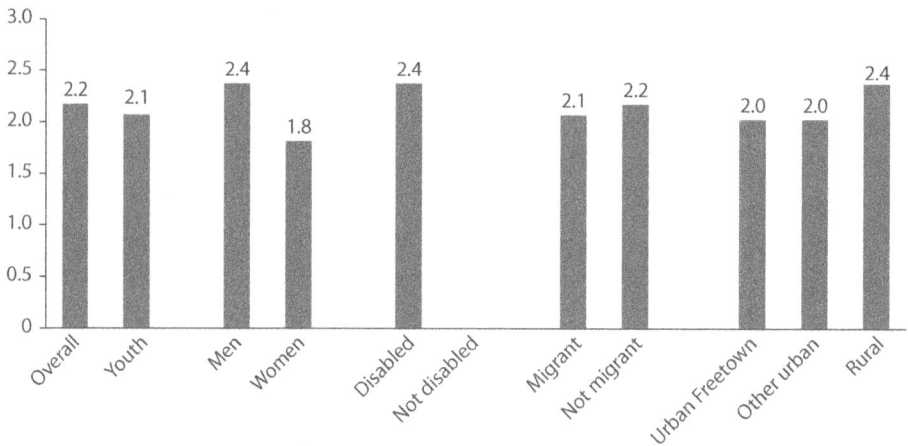

Source: 2014 Sierra Leone Labor Force Survey.

across population groups is generally limited, although, among people who enroll in vocational training, men spend an average of nearly seven months more in training than women (figure 2.9). Similarly, among people who receive training, rural residents invest an extra five months relative to urban dwellers.

People who have never attended school or who have obtained technical degrees or certificates spend the most time in vocational training. Among people who have undertaken vocational training, those who have never attended school have acquired an average of 2.4 years of training, while those with tertiary degrees, the highest level of education, have obtained 1.9 years (figure 2.10). Because 66.4 percent of the rural working-age population has never attended formal education institutions (see figure 2.2), the extra training shown in figure 2.9 among this group may be helping compensate for a lack of formal education

Figure 2.10 Average Years of Training among Trainees, by Educational Attainment and Province

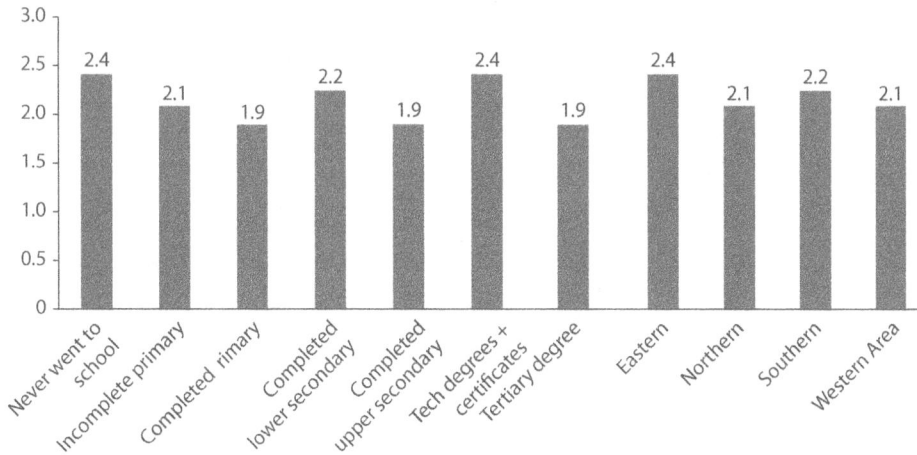

Source: 2014 Sierra Leone Labor Force Survey.

Table 2.1 Initial and Final Years of Formal Education and Years of Training

Education Before Training Start	Final Years of Education	Years of Training
None	7.3	3.4
Primary Incomplete	4.7	2.4
Primary Completed	7.3	2.9
Secondary Incomplete	10.1	2.3
Secondary Completed	12.9	2.3

Source: 2014 Sierra Leone Labor Force Survey.

in rural areas. A similar logic may hold among the disabled, among whom 70.9 percent have not received formal schooling.

Individuals who undertook vocational training even before attending formal educational institutions had the longest training spells. Individuals who undertook vocational training even before attending formal educational institutions had the longest training spells, an average of 3.4 years (table 2.1).[5] However, they went on to obtain an average additional 7.3 years of formal education after starting the training courses. Likewise, people who undertook vocational training after starting, but not completing primary school followed the training courses an average of 2.4 years, but went on to obtain much less additional formal education. This suggests, again, that vocational training is used, at least in part, to compensate for a lack of formal education.

Individuals who have obtained a greater average number of years of vocational training tend to earn less than individuals with fewer average years of training. People with less than a year of vocational training have median earnings of Le 930,000 a year, while people with more than four years of vocational training earn Le 430,000 less per year (figure 2.11). Given that indi-

Findings from the 2014 Labor Force Survey in Sierra Leone
http://dx.doi.org/10.1596/978-1-4648-0742-8

Figure 2.11   Median Earnings, by Average Years of Vocational Training

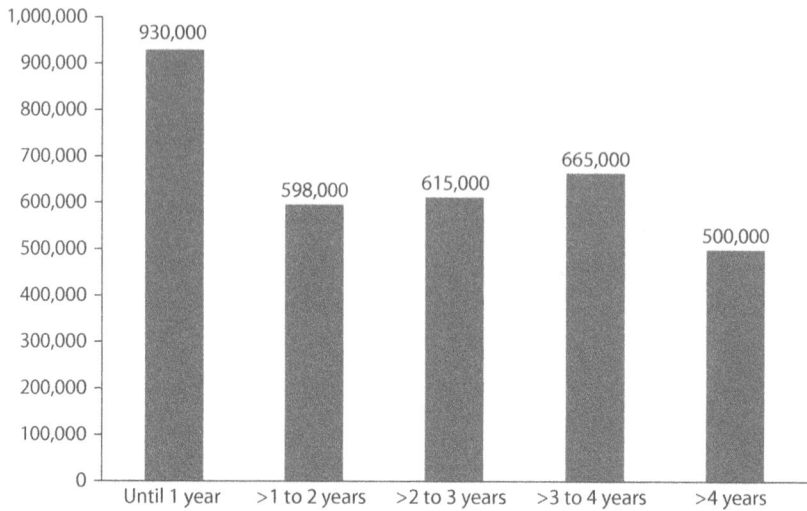

Source: 2014 Sierra Leone Labor Force Survey.

viduals with the least formal educational attainment tend to spend the most time in vocational training, these results suggest that additional years of vocational training may not be sufficient in terms of earnings to offset a lack of formal education.

Fields of Study and Certification

Not all areas of vocational training are accessible to the least well-educated workers, and the choice of field is closely determined by the level of formal education obtained before undertaking the training. None of the people who had never attended formal schooling enrolled in training in teaching or business services, whereas 47 percent of these people undertook training in construction and manufacturing, and 41 percent took personal services training (figure 2.12). Meanwhile, people who had completed secondary school before starting vocational training were distributed more evenly across vocational areas: 22 percent trained in business services, 14 percent in nursing, and 19 percent each in in the teaching profession and in construction and manufacturing; personal services accounted for 17 percent, and even agriculture was pursued by 2 percent of secondary school graduates.

The years of training needed for the various certificates vary slightly around an average of 2.3 years. A teaching certificate requires an average of 2.9 years of training; a nursing diploma, an average of 2.7 years; an agricultural diploma, 2.4 years (figure 2.13). Individuals who quit training programs without certificates did so after an average of 2.3 years.

Training lasts an average of 1.3–3.1 years, depending on the subject.[6] Automobile and motorcycle mechanics (3.1 years) and teacher training (2.7

Figure 2.12 Fields of Study, by Formal Educational Attainment prior to Undertaking Vocational Training

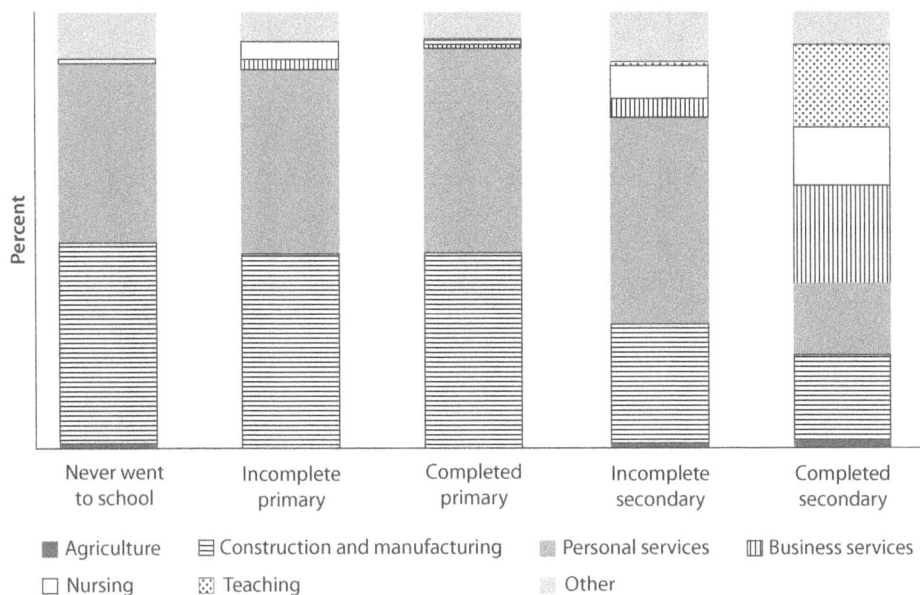

Source: 2014 Sierra Leone Labor Force Survey.
Note: Business services include training in business services and computer and Internet services. Construction and manufacturing include training as electrical technicians or in plumbing, carpentry, masonry, blacksmithing, or gara (tie dyeing). Personal services include automobile and motorcycle mechanics, tailoring, hairdressing, and catering.

Figure 2.13 Average Number of Years to Earn Training Certification

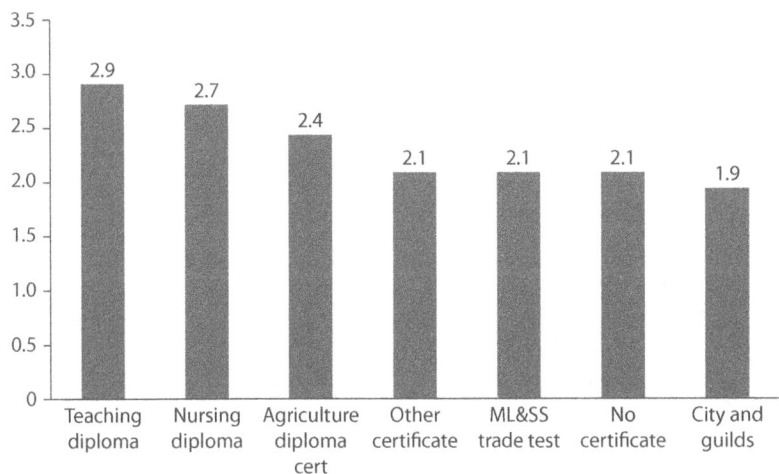

Source: 2014 Sierra Leone Labor Force Survey.

years) take the longest (figure 2.14). Computer and Internet services (1.3 years), gara tie dyeing (1.7 years), and hairdressing (1.9 years) require the fewest years. Because the average number of years spent in training in certain fields (nursing, teaching) is less than the average number of years needed to obtain certification, many people clearly start training, but drop out before certification.

Findings from the 2014 Labor Force Survey in Sierra Leone
http://dx.doi.org/10.1596/978-1-4648-0742-8

Figure 2.14 Average Years of Training, by Field

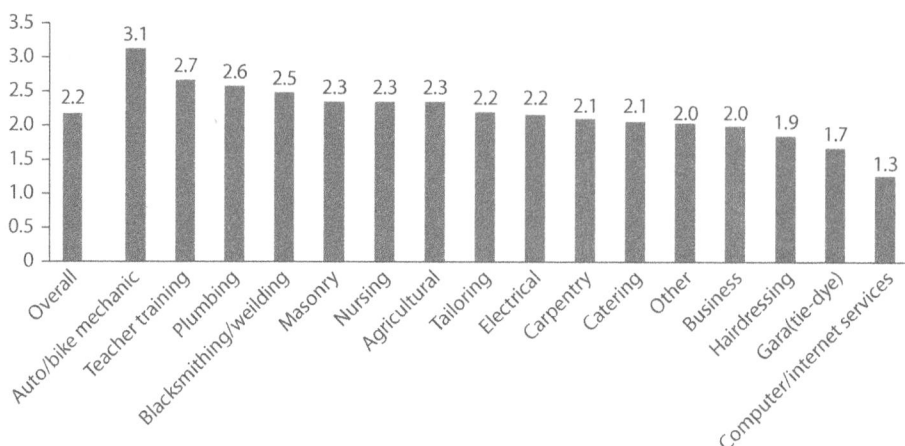

Source: 2014 Sierra Leone Labor Force Survey.

Figure 2.15 Training Areas, by Characteristics of Individuals and Province

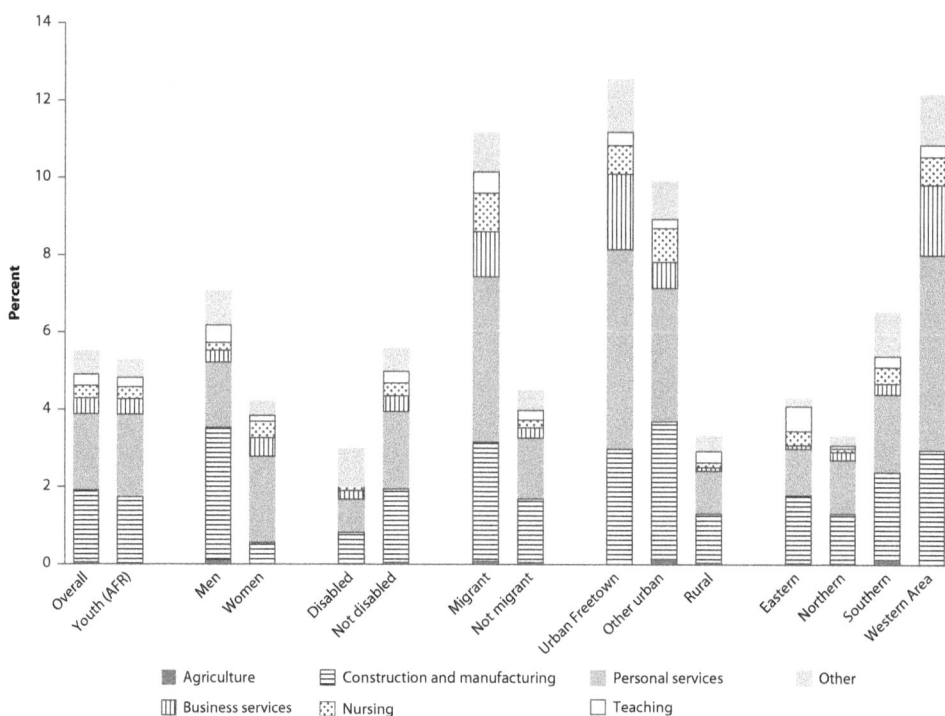

Source: 2014 Sierra Leone Labor Force Survey.

Men and women generally undertake training in completely different areas (figure 2.15). The most common areas among men are carpentry, masonry, and automobile–motorcycle mechanics, but these areas are among the least common among women. Catering, hairdressing, and gara tie dyeing are rarely chosen by men, but they are among the most common areas among women. Tailoring is the area select-ed the most by women (21.5 percent of all trained women), and 11.4 percent of men also undertake training in this area. The clear gender differentiation across fields reflects the envi-ronment in which young people make their training decisions, as well as personal preferences and social expectations. This early separation between men and women across fields of training has the potential to widen the gender wage gap because men focus on areas that are associ-ated with higher earnings.[7]

Apprenticeship

Among the working-age population, 6.4 percent have served as apprentices; the share is higher among men, migrants, and urban residents (figure 2.16). The share of men who have been apprentices is nearly 4.5 times higher than the share of women (11.1 percent vs. 2.5 percent), while migrants are nearly twice as likely as nonmigrants to have served as apprentices (10.7 percent vs. 5.6 percent). More individuals have been apprentices in urban Freetown than in other areas, which may be caused by a limited supply of apprenticeship opportunities in rural areas or the possibility that an apprenticeship is not considered as worthwhile in rural areas.

Similar to vocational training, men and women choose radically different trades as appren-tices. The favorite trades among men are the least common among women, for example car-pentry, automobile and motorcycle mechanics, and masonry (figure 2.17). Similarly, in two of the most common trades among women, catering and hairdressing, men are practically absent. As with vocational training, tailoring is a profession that is highly sought after by women, while men also engage in it, but to a lesser extent (20.6 percent of all apprenticeships among women vs. 9.7 percent among men). Agricultural apprenticeships seem to be the second most common trade among women, accounting for 20.3 percent of women who serve as appren-tices; men do not engage in this trade. As with vocational training, determining factors in the gender differentiation across apprenticeships likely include social norms, preferences, and opportunities, though the data do not allow testing of these hypotheses.

Figure 2.16 Working-Age Population Undertaking Apprenticeships, by Characteristics of Individuals

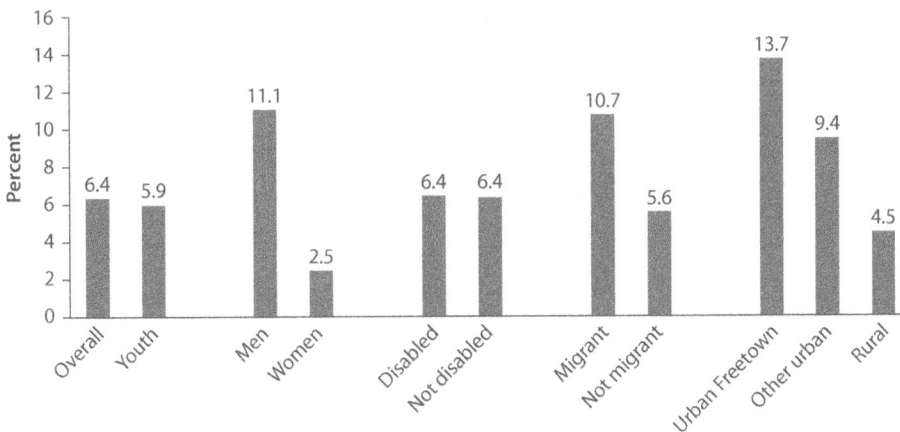

Source: 2014 Sierra Leone Labor Force Survey.

Findings from the 2014 Labor Force Survey in Sierra Leone
http://dx.doi.org/10.1596/978-1-4648-0742-8

Figure 2.17 Apprenticeship Trades, by Gender

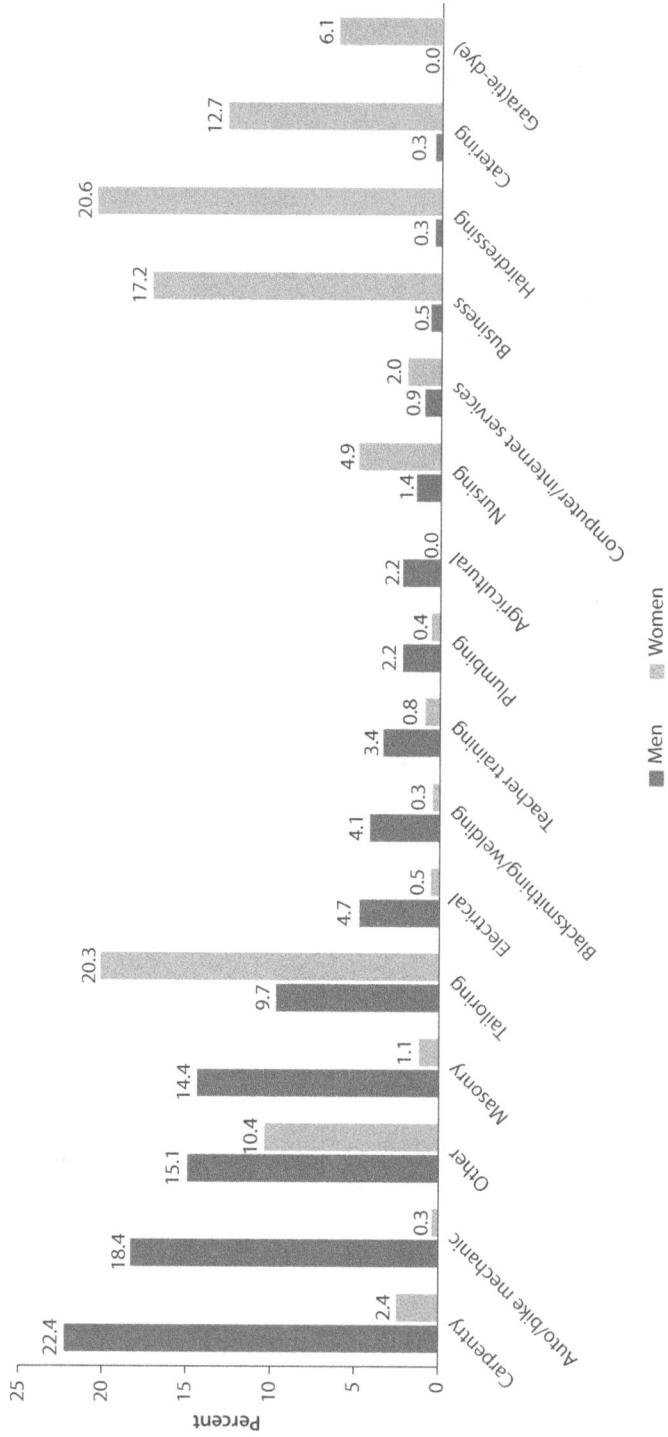

Source: 2014 Sierra Leone Labor Force Survey.

Skills and Earnings

Overall, earnings increase with educational attainment, but most of the variation is in the tails of the distribution. Median labor earnings are lowest among individuals who have never attended school, and, among individuals who have incomplete primary school, they are nearly double (a 98 percent increase) compared with median earnings among those with no schooling (see chapter 1 and table B.3). There is relatively little variation in earnings between incomplete primary school and completed upper-secondary school. Nonetheless, labor earnings more than triple among people with postsecondary degrees relative to people with upper-secondary degrees.

One must obtain a certificate or diploma to see a significant earnings gain from vocational training, and there is no significant boost to median earnings associated with serving an apprenticeship. Overall, median earnings were Le 618,000 among individuals who underwent vocational training programs and Le 600,000 among individuals who did not undergo training. Median earnings were Le 600,000 among individuals whether they had or had not served in apprenticeships. However, among those who received vocational training, obtaining a certificate is associated with higher earnings, and certificates of the Ministry of Labor and Social Security are associated with the highest earnings (figure 2.18). Individuals who have undergone training, but who have not obtained certificates earn significantly less than individuals who obtain certificates. Training certificates of the Ministry of Labor and Social Security are associated with median earnings that are around 50 percent higher relative to teaching diplomas.

Figure 2.18   Median Earnings, by Type of Vocational Training Certificate

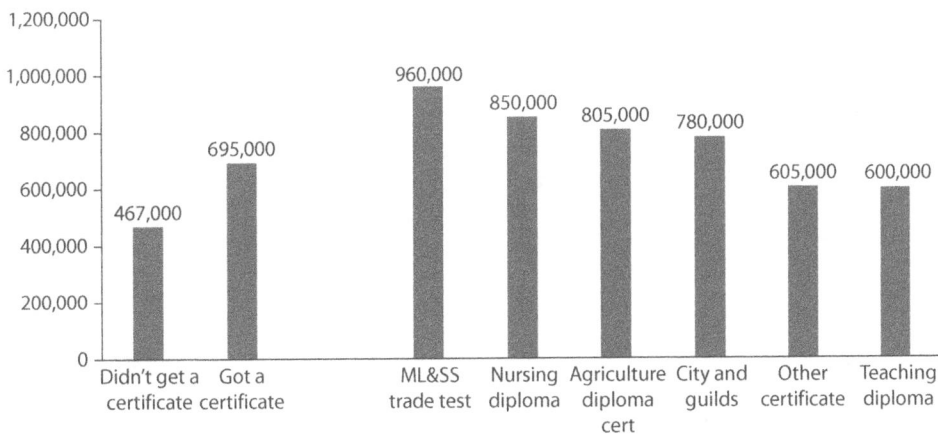

Source: 2014 Sierra Leone Labor Force Survey.

Findings from the 2014 Labor Force Survey in Sierra Leone
http://dx.doi.org/10.1596/978-1-4648-0742-8

Notes

1. The remaining 3.1 percent of the people with no education are distributed as follows: 2.0 percent can read and write; 1.0 percent can read only; and 0.1 percent can write only.

2. Years of schooling have been calculated by converting specific educational levels to years of schooling. For details on how the years of schooling variable has been created, see the last cell in appendix A, table A.1.

3. The Sierra Leone Labor Force Survey (SLLFS) questionnaire does not distinguish between government-owned and government-assisted schools.

4. For the calculation of years of vocational training, observations reporting six years or more of training (around 5 percent of the observations for the variable) have been dropped. This was so for three reasons. First, there is a possibility that respondents confused months and years. Second, there may have been coding errors. Third, it is unlikely that a training program lasts more than five years.

5. Only 13 sampled individuals undertook training before starting school; thus, this average has been calculated based on the SLLFS is an imprecise estimate of the true number of years of additional education and of training.

6. These calculations are based on few observations. The number of observations ranges from 13 to 133 for the areas of training; so, the results must be used with caution.

7. Some types of jobs in which men tend disproportionately to specialize, such as construction, are generally associated with higher wages than jobs in fields chosen predominately by women, such as services, but the inverse is true if the individual undertakes a job as a self-employed nonagricultural worker (see chapter 1).

CHAPTER 3

Farming Activities and Nonfarm Household Enterprises

In Sierra Leone, farm and nonfarm household enterprises employ large shares of the population; respectively, 59.2 percent and 31.4 percent of employed individuals report them as their main activities. The remaining 9.5 percent are wage employees. Given the importance of farm and nonfarm household enterprises, the factors related with the productivity of these enterprises should be explored.

Farming Activities

The majority of households and the employed within them are engaged in agricultural activities; among these workers, women constitute a larger share than men. At least one member in most households (72.8 percent) is involved in the agricultural activities of the household enterprise (photo 3.1). Among all employed working-age individuals, 61.1 percent work in agriculture, fishing, or forestry; the share of women in agricultural employment is slightly higher than the share of men (53.5 percent vs. 46.5 percent). The vast majority of these are self-employed; only 3.1 percent are in wage work.[1] The share of women in agricultural self-employment is similar to the corresponding share among all agricultural workers (54.0 percent women vs. 46.0 percent men).

However, in terms of hours worked, men carry a larger burden in agricultural activities than women. The working-age agricultural self-employed work an average of 43.8 hours a week in their main employment, and those whose secondary economic activity is agricultural self-employment work an average of 23.8 hours a week. Men engaged in agricultural self-employment as their main job work significantly more hours than women (45.6 hours vs. 42.3 hours), as do those who are engaged in these jobs as a secondary employment (26.1 hours among men vs. 21.9 hours among women).

Educational attainment is less among agricultural workers than among the overall working-age population. Around 67.5 percent of the working-age population have never attended school, while a much higher share of the

Photo 3.1   A group of young men mills rice at a processing center in Kabala Town

Photo Credit: Andrea Martin.

Table 3.1   Educational Attainment among Self-Employed Agricultural Workers

Education level	Working-age population			Agricultural self-employed		
	Overall	Men	Women	Overall	Men	Women
Never went to school	67.5	58.0	75.4	80.0	72.8	86.1
Incomplete primary	6.1	6.3	5.9	5.2	6.0	4.6
Completed primary	9.3	11.0	7.9	7.2	9.1	5.6
Completed lower secondary	8.6	11.4	6.3	5.1	7.0	3.5
Completed upper secondary	5.8	9.4	2.8	2.2	4.5	0.2
Tech degrees + certificates	2.0	2.7	1.4	0.3	0.7	
Tertiary degree	0.7	1.2	0.3			
Total	100	100	100	100	100	100

Source: 2014 Sierra Leone Labor Force Survey.

working-age agricultural self-employed (80.0 percent) have never attended
school (table 3.1). A similar pattern is observed across genders: men and
women in agricultural self-employment have less education relative to the
overall population. The gender gap is also slightly wider in agricultural self-
employment than among overall working-age population: the difference

between the share of men and women who have never attended school in the overall working-age population is 17.4 percent compared with 13.3 percent among the agricultural self-employed.

Untitled ownership of agricultural land is common, particularly outside Freetown. The vast majority of plots are owned (75.1 percent). However, despite the high level of reported plot ownership, more than half the plots reported as owned (61.3 percent) are not associated with title documents; only 31.3 percent are associated with land titles; 6.5 percent are associated with traditional certificates; and the rest (around 1.0 percent) are associated with other documents proving ownership (table 3.2). Tenure security, as proxied by possession of a land title, proof of sale, or other document, is significantly more common in Freetown. This is consistent with the dual land tenure system in the country. Outside the Western Area, most plots remain under customary law whereby chiefs serve as custodians of the land, which is held in the name of lineages, families, and individuals, and sales are prohibited beyond the family or community (USAID 2013) (table 3.3).[2]

Table 3.2 Proof of Landownership

	Overall	Freetown	Other urban	Rural
No document	61.3	15.8	65	61.2
Land title	31.3	41.7	22.0	32.0
Traditional certificate	6.5	4.9	10.9	6.1
Proof of sale	0.4	23.1	1.3	0.2
Other documents	0.6	14.6	0.8	0.5
Total	100	100	100	100

Source: 2014 Sierra Leone Labor Force Survey.

Table 3.3 Ownership Status of Plots

	All Sierra Leone	Urban Freetown	Other urban	Rural	Eastern	Northern	Southern	Western Area
Owned	75.1	52.5	73.0	75.4	84.1	70.9	75.7	39.9
Rented in (from someone for pay)	9.3	25.0	12.6	9.0	6.3	9.4	12.2	26.5
Mortgaged	0.1	5.3	0.3	0.1	0.1	0.1	0.2	2.8
Borrowed for free (no need to pay back)	10.8	14.1	9.9	10.8	4.3	15.6	6.6	23.3
Common land	4.2	3.1	4.0	4.2	5.2	3.9	3.8	3.5
Other	0.4	0.0	0.2	0.4	0.0	0.0	1.6	4.0
Total	100	100	100	100	100	100	100	100

Source: 2014 Sierra Leone Labor Force Survey.

The rental market for agricultural land is limited, though it is more common in the Western Area. Overall, 9.3 percent of plots are rented. In the Western Area, the share is higher: around a quarter of plots (26.5 percent) are rented. In other urban and in rural areas, where agricultural activity is more prevalent, land rental occurs less frequently (12.6 percent and 9.0 of plots, respectively). Around 10.8 percent of plots are borrowed at no cost. The share is also higher in the Western Area (23.3 percent). Both these findings are also consistent with the dual land tenure system and may also be reinforced by local customs, but, to the extent the landless do not have flexible, lower-cost options to gain access to land, this may have implications for productivity.

Most plots are owned by men; women typically own smaller plots. Of all plots, 67.8 percent are owned by men, 20.7 percent are owned by women, and 11.6 percent are owned by households. The average size of plots is 9.4 acres. Plots in urban Freetown are an average of 1.1 acres; in rural areas, 9.4 acres; and, in other urban areas, 10.4 acres.[3] Plots owned by women are smaller than those owned by men (8.3 acres vs. 11.1 acres). Older people (36–64 age group) own larger plots relative to youth (15–35) (12.0 acres vs. 8.0 acres).

Most agricultural workers have limited access to technology, inputs, credit, and extension services, which are positively correlated with farming profits. Only 5.5 percent of agricultural workers live in households in which mechanical equipment is used, and those who do live in such households tend to work large plots (the average plot size is 17.6 acres).[4] Only 4.6 percent of agricultural workers live in households that have access to extension worker services for farming activities. More than half of plots (63.9 percent) have no irrigation systems; among those that have irrigation systems, the main water source is a waterway (61.3 percent).[5] On the vast majority of plots, no fertilizers or pesticides are used. On most plots (65.5 percent), no fertilizers are used, and no payment for fertilizers is associated with 23.8 percent plots.[6] Among those plots on which purchased fertilizers are used, the median expenditure is Le 150,000. On 77.6 percent of plots, no pesticides are used, and, on 21.6 percent of plots, pesticides are used, but these are not purchased. Among those plots for which pesticides are purchased, the median expenditure is Le 6,000. In contrast, seeds are purchased for two-thirds of plots (69.2 percent); seeds are obtained free of charge for the remainder, likely as a by-product of the previous harvest. Among those plots for which seeds have been purchased, the median expenditure is Le 120,000.

Almost 40 percent of agricultural workers live in households that face credit constraints, and agricultural workers in households benefiting from more capital are less credit constrained.[7] Agricultural workers who live in households that own plots, that are able to hire outside labor, that use mechanical equipment, or that have access to extension services are considerably less credit constrained than those that do not possess such capital. The link between landownership and credit constraints likely arises because of the ability of households that own plots to use land as collateral, although only 32.5 percent of individuals live in landowning households that hold land titles. Among all agricultural workers who live in households that hire outside labor, 36.4 percent care credit constrained, while 53.2 percent of agricultural workers who live in households that do not hire outside labor are credit constrained (figure 3.1). The particularly high share of agricultural workers who are credit constrained and who own farms that do not have access to extension services suggests there may be an opportunity to improve the productivity of agriculture by reducing the cost of extension services. A similar argument may also hold in considering the use of mechanical equipment.

Households with larger plots tend to enjoy higher agricultural profits and to be slightly less likely to be credit constrained. The correlation between land size and agricultural profits is positive (0.2174). The plots on which people whose agricultural work is performed for households subject to credit constraints are an average of 6.4 acres smaller than the plots of households that are not credit constrained (19.6 acres vs. 13.2 acres). Among individuals, however, land size and credit constraints are slightly negatively correlated (−0.0848). These results suggest that larger plots may be associated with the application of more productive technologies, which render these plots or the revenues they generate useful as collateral for loans. The extra profits and lower credit constraints associated with larger plots are not, however, driven by education: there is a negative correlation between land size and years of education (−0.072).

Households that spent more on seeds and fertilizers tended to be more well educated, saw higher agricultural profits, and faced narrower credit constraints. Agricultural profits are more strongly correlated with the total cost of seeds (0.253) than with the total cost of fertilizers (0.158). These results suggest that credit constraints may be preventing some households from investing in more expensive, more productive seeds (correlation −0.052) and fertilizers (correlation −0.059) and that, in the absence of these constraints, household incomes might increase. Similarly, years of education are positively correlated with the total cost of seeds (0.035) and the total cost of fertilizers (0.019), suggesting that more well-educated individuals may be able to more well understand the longer-term benefits of investing in more expensive seeds and fertilizers.

Figure 3.1 **Share of Agricultural Workers with Credit Constraints, by Farm Characteristics**

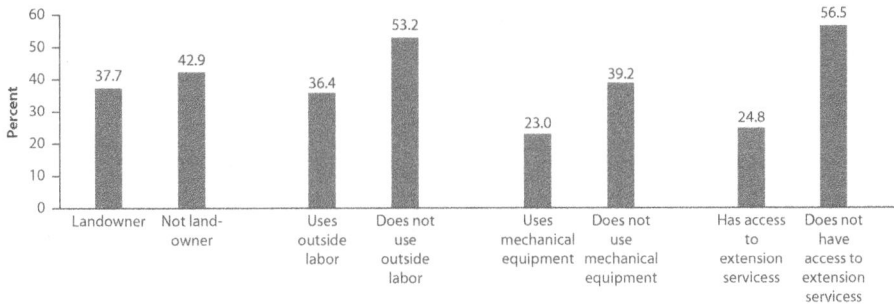

Source: 2014 Sierra Leone Labor Force Survey.

Findings from the 2014 Labor Force Survey in Sierra Leone
http://dx.doi.org/10.1596/978-1-4648-0742-8

Figure 3.2 Median Value of Agricultural Output (in Leones), by Farm Characteristics

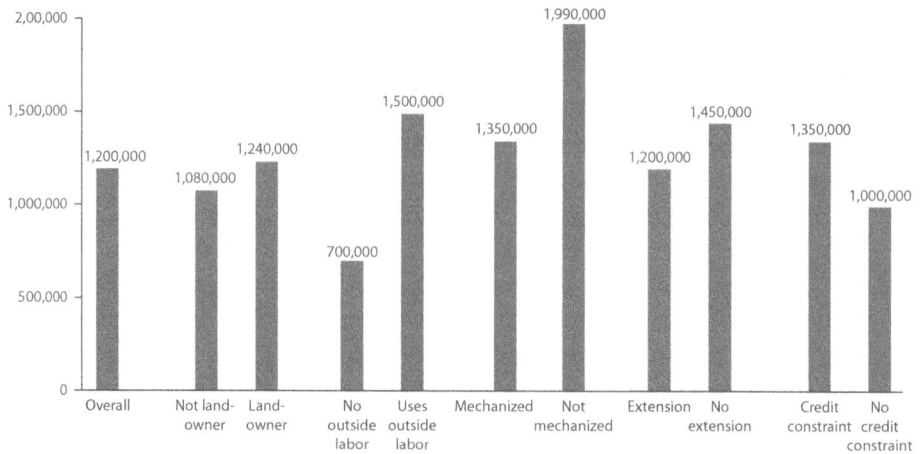

Source: 2014 Sierra Leone Labor Force Survey.

The estimated monetary value of agricultural output is higher among farms that have better access to capital (figure 3.2). The estimated monetary value of output is more than double among farms that use outside labor than among farms that do not use outside labor. The median value of outputs is considerably higher among farms that are owned by households, that hire outside labor, that use mechanical equipment, and that have access to extension services than among counterparts. The value of output is higher among farms that do not face credit constraints than among farms that face credit constraints (Le 1,350,000 vs. Le 1,000,000).

Nonfarm Household Enterprises

Nonfarm household enterprises[8] constitute the second-largest source of jobs in the economy, and a greater share of this labor is provided by women (photo 3.2). About half of all households (49.6 percent) report that they have at least one member working in nonagricultural self-employment.[9] Restricting this to only households that have at least one member employed in nonagricultural self-employment as their main job, the percentage is lower, but still one-third of households (37.2 percent). Women represent a larger share (63.8 percent) of the working age employed in nonagricultural self-employment as their main job. Similarly, within the household, women represent 61.7 percent of those who report being engaged in nonagricultural activities.[10]

A nonnegligent proportion of households in Sierra Leone diversify labor across farm and nonfarm self-employment. Among households with at least one member of working age employed in nonagricultural self-employment, 26.1 percent also have one agricultural self-employed worker. The variations

Photo 3.2 A woman displays a range of colorful fabrics at her shop in Koidu Town

Photo Credit: Andrea Martin.

across areas are wide; the share is 42 percent in rural areas, 8.4 percent in other urban areas, and only 0.1 percent in Freetown. At the individual level, combining different jobs over short periods of time is similarly common: 22.6 percent of nonfarm household enterprise workers report that they had engaged in a secondary job in the last week.[11] The majority combine farm and nonfarm self-employment: among those working in nonfarm self-employment as their main economic activity who have a secondary economic activity, 83.6 percent report agricultural self-employment as their secondary economic activity.

Most household enterprises are microenterprises, but men tend to own slightly larger enterprises than women and are more likely to hire labor. The average number of workers is 1.7. Among enterprises, 66.7 percent have only one worker; 20.2 percent have two workers; and less than 15 percent have three or more workers.[12] Female-owned enterprises have an average of 1.6 workers in total, while male-owned enterprises have 1.9 workers in total, a small but statistically significant difference. Only 3.1 percent of the enterprises hire paid workers from outside the household, and, on average, most workers tend to be from within the household (an average of 1.5 workers from within the household compared with 0.2 workers from outside the household). Female-owned enterprises are less likely than male-owned enterprises to hire outside labor (1.6 percent vs. 5.4 percent). Among household enterprises that hire labor, female-owned

Findings from the 2014 Labor Force Survey in Sierra Leone
http://dx.doi.org/10.1596/978-1-4648-0742-8

enterprises hire fewer laborers relative to male-owned enterprises (an average of 0.08 workers vs. 0.34 workers).

The nonagricultural self-employed typically work more hours per week relative to the agricultural self-employed. Those among whom nonagricultural self-employment is the main economic activity work an average of 46.4 hours a week, while those among whom agricultural self-employment is the main activity work around 3.0 hours less per week (43.8 hours). A similar pattern is observed in analyzing workers with secondary economic activities: among these, the nonagricultural self-employed work an average of 19.8 hours a week, and the agricultural self-employed work 19.8 hours a week.

The educational attainment of those working in nonfarm household enterprises is similar to that of the overall population, but greater than the educational attainment of self-employed agricultural workers. More than half of those working in nonfarm enterprises (59.9 percent) have no education, which is lower than in the overall working-age employed population (67.5 percent).[13] Almost none (0.3 percent) of those working in nonfarm enterprises have tertiary degrees. The years of education are also similar among nonfarm enterprise workers and the overall population (8.7 years vs. 8.4 years). Nonfarm enterprise workers are more well educated than self-employed agricultural workers: 59.9 percent of nonfarm enterprise workers have no education compared with 80.0 percent among self-employed agricultural workers. And nonfarm enterprise workers have an average of around one year more of education relative to self-employed farm workers (8.4 years vs. 7.6 years).

Most household enterprises are traders or shopkeepers who do not operate in fixed locations.[14] The location of a business can have implications for business practices, access to credit, security risks related to investments, and other factors associated with profitability. Nonfarm household enterprises in Sierra Leone tend to have a variable location (42.1 percent) or are located within the home (37.6 percent); only 20.3 percent have fixed locations outside the home. As a result, only one-fifth (19.8 percent) of jobs in household enterprises are in fixed locations outside the home. To a certain extent, this is consistent with the nature of the typical activities of these enterprises: an average of 84.0 percent of household enterprises are trader or shopkeeper enterprises; 9.9 percent provide services; and 6.2 percent are producers. However, there is not much variation in the types of enterprise across the location of activities, suggesting that this may be a broader business constraint.

Nonagricultural self-employed workers who work in household enterprises that have permanent locations are less likely to face credit constraints.[15] An average of 46.7 percent of individuals who work in nonfarm household enterprises find that their enterprise credit is constrained. This share is lower (40.9 percent) among those individuals whose nonfarm household enterprises have permanent locations outside the home, and higher among those individuals working in enterprises with a variable location (46.6 percent) or among those who work in enterprises located within a home (51.0 percent).[16] These differences in credit constraints may influence the location of a nonfarm household enterprise activity, for instance, if the credit-constrained enterprises are not able to secure funds to rent or purchase a permanent site or the equipment for a mobile location. Conversely, the lack of a permanent business location may be the reason these nonfarm household enterprises are less likely to be able to secure extra capital. In addition, workers in household enterprises in permanent locations outside the home have higher levels of educational attainment than workers in enterprises in the home and workers in enterprises with variable locations (8.4, 8.0, and 7.1, respectively). This may indicate that the more well educated are better at circumventing the constraints associated with establishing business locations, for example, through better acquaintanceship networks or higher creditworthiness.

The availability of larger amounts of start-up capital is associated with higher revenues and profits. For the group that invests up to 40,000 at start-up, revenue at the time of the survey was Le 745,000. The revenue increases as the amount of start-up capital rises: the group with start-up capital greater than Le 1 million has a revenue of Le 7,578,000, which is more than 10 times the revenue obtained by those who invested up to Le 40,000. A similar positive relationship is found between start-up capital and profits (figure 3.3), which reflects the size of operations that more initial capital allows, as well as other factors—such as socioeconomic position—that can affect both the availability of capital and firm performance. Taking the total number of workers as a proxy for size, enterprise size tends to increase with the start-up capital invested. Those enterprises that invested the least start-up capital (up to Le 40,000) had

Figure 3.3 Median Household Enterprise Profits, by Amount of Start-Up Capital

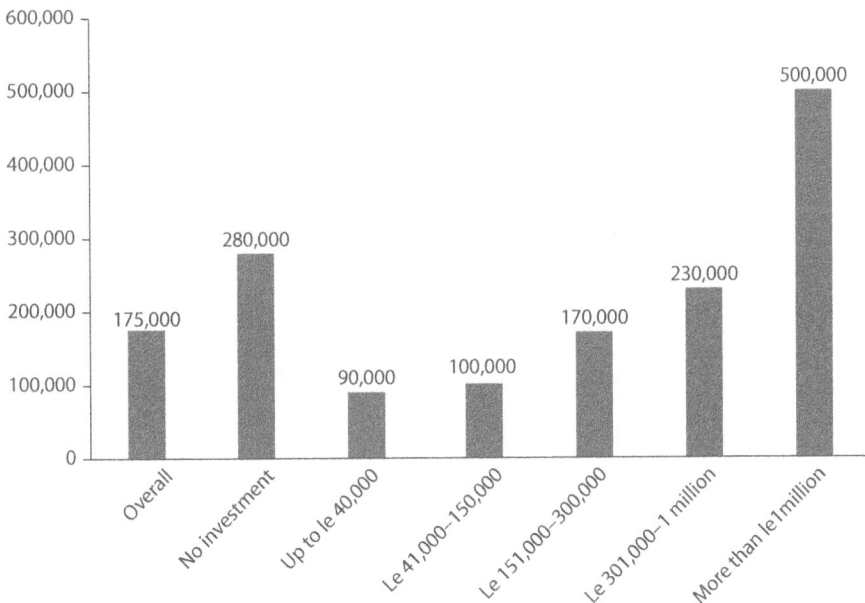

Source: 2014 Sierra Leone Labor Force Survey.

Findings from the 2014 Labor Force Survey in Sierra Leone
http://dx.doi.org/10.1596/978-1-4648-0742-8

an average of 1.6 workers, while those that invested more than Le 1 million had an average of 2.1 workers. Both revenues and profits are higher among enterprises with no start-up investment; however, this is likely because this group includes individuals who inherited the family business.

The main source of start-up capital is family and friends. Among all enterprises, 38.6 percent obtained their start-up capital from family and friends. Among all enterprises, 32.9 percent used the savings of the owner to start-up the business, and 19.7 percent used the proceeds from other businesses to start up. The role of the financial sector seems to be limited because only 2.9 percent of nonfarm household enterprises obtained their start-up capital through a money-lender, microfinance institution, or bank. This implies that there is a large scope for financial institutions to provide services that cater to potential entrepreneurs so as to assure a more stable enterprise financing source than family and friends.

The vast majority of household enterprise workers work in enterprises that do not keep formal financial records (85.6 percent). Only 10.1 percent of workers work in enterprises that follow good business practices and keep financial records separate from household financial records (figure 3.4). Those who work in enterprises with a permanent location are more likely (14.5 percent of enterprise workers) to be working in enterprises that keep financial records separated from household financial records. Those working in enterprises located in their homes are less likely than those in enterprises with variable location to be working in an enterprise that keeps separated records (8.0 percent vs. 10.5 percent).

Figure 3.4 Financial Records of Household Enterprise by Household Enterprise Location

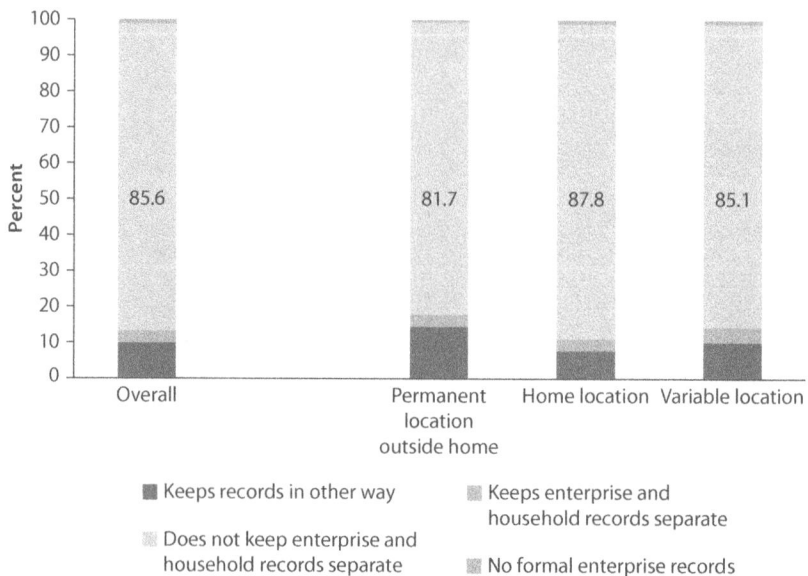

Source: 2014 Sierra Leone Labor Force Survey.

There are notable differences in household enterprise profits across geographical areas and the gender of the enterprise owners. Overall, the median profit across operating enterprises is Le 100,000. Women are more heavily concentrated in nonfarm self-employment (see above); yet, the median monthly profits of man-owned enterprises are almost double the profits of woman-owned enterprises (Le 80,000 vs. Le 140,000).[17] Nonfarm enterprises in Freetown are the most profitable: in Freetown, the median monthly revenue is Le 200,000, nearly triple the amounts in other urban areas (Le 70,000) and double the amounts in rural areas (Le 95,000). Somewhat surprisingly, there are no noticeable differences in median revenue between enterprises owned by youth and older people; they both have median monthly revenues of Le 100,000. Further analysis is needed to understand how differences in the factors discussed above influence these gaps in profits.

Notes

1. Of the employed working-age population, 59.2 percent are in agricultural self-employment; 31.3 percent are in nonagricultural self-employment; and 9.5 percent are in wage employment.

2. USAID (United States Agency for International Development) (2013), "USAID Country Profile: Property Rights and Resource Governance, Sierra Leone," http://usaidlandtenure.net/sites/default/files/country-profiles/full-reports/USAID_Land_Tenure_Sierra_Leone_Profile.pdf.

3. This excludes land that was not cultivated during the previous growing season.

4. Mechanical equipment includes tractors, harvesters, and so on.

5. Waterways include rivers and lakes. Other irrigation methods are wells (14.7 percent of plots), rain (12.7 percent), drilling (8.5 percent), and dams or impoundments (2.9 percent).

6. Fertilizers include organic fertilizers (such as manure and compost) and inorganic or chemical fertilizers.

7. Credit constrained means that an individual or household is unable to borrow money for household farming activities either in normal circumstances or if a negative shock affects the household.

8. In this section, nonfarm household enterprise workers are defined as working-age household members who owned or were engaged in nonfarm household enterprises in the 12 months previous to the survey.

9. Households that reported that they operated any nonagricultural income-generating enterprise that produces goods or services or that they have anyone in the household who owned a shop or operated a trading business.

10. The survey asks about up to 10 household members who are engaged in nonfarm household enterprises. Hence, the comparison may not be with all the employed population.

11. This may not adequately reflect how activities are combined during the peak seasons for agricultural work, as the survey period coincides with the beginning of the lean season.

12. Only 7.2 percent have three workers, and 5.9 percent have four or more workers.

Findings from the 2014 Labor Force Survey in Sierra Leone
http://dx.doi.org/10.1596/978-1-4648-0742-8

13. The share of individuals in working age (without restricting only to those who are employed) who have no education is 55.2 percent, which is the same number reported in map 2.1.

14. A home location refers to enterprises that operate within the homes of the business owners, with or without a special business space. A permanent location refers to a separate structure, a permanent nonresidential building, or a fixed stall in a market or street. A variable location refers to enterprises that operate from vehicles, carts, temporary stalls in markets or streets, construction sites, the homes of clients, and other such locations.

15. Constrained borrowing is defined as not being able to borrow money for the household enterprise, in regular situations or when a negative shock affects the household enterprise.

16. The difference in borrowing constraints between enterprises with permanent locations outside the home and enterprises without such a permanent location is statistically significant.

17. Total profits that the enterprise normally earns per month in the last 12 months.

CHAPTER 4

Informality

This chapter describes informality in the wage sector. Formality is important not only for the conditions that formal employment offers workers but also for tax collection and the potential effects of formality on productivity (Photo 4.1).

Informality is pervasive in Sierra Leone; over 35 percent of wage jobs and over 88 percent of nonagricultural self-employment are informal.[1] Formal wage jobs are most often formal because employers offer relevant written contracts to employees (91 percent of wage jobs), although the employers in the case of nearly three-quarters of formal jobs also deduct income taxes or contribute to related pension or retirement funds (table 4.1). Paid leave and medical benefits are the least common reasons for classifying jobs as formal; less than half of formal wage jobs are associated with either of these benefits. Wage jobs that meet one criterion of formality often meet several other criteria as well.

Among wage employees, formal jobs are considered good jobs. These jobs are considered better than informal jobs primarily because the workers in these jobs earn more, on average, than informal wage workers (Le 2.25 million a month vs. Le 1.99 million). Moreover, formal wage workers most often simultaneously receive multiple benefits. However, formal wage workers tend to be more well educated than informal wage workers (average of 12.2 years of education vs. 8.5 years), suggesting that access to these jobs may not be open to all workers.[2]

The share of formal wage jobs is more than five times larger than the share of jobs in registered household enterprises involved in nonagricultural self-employment (figure 4.1). Women are much more likely than men to be formally employed if they are in wage work (74 percent vs. 61 percent), although a larger share of men work in registered enterprises involved in nonagricultural self-employment activities (21 percent vs. 8 percent among women). Formality increases with educational attainment in both wage employment and nonagricultural self-employment: the highest rates of formality are among workers with tertiary degrees. Workers with tertiary degrees are more than

Photo 4.1 A male tailor in Western Rural puts the finishing touches on a garment

Photo Credit: Samantha Zaldivar.

Table 4.1 Criteria of Formality, Wage Jobs

	Written contract (%)	Income tax deducted from wages (%)	Employer contributions to a pension/ retirement fund (%)	Paid leave (%)	Medical benefits (%)	Overall (%)
Written contract	100.0	73.2	70.2	47.5	43.4	90.7
Income tax deducted from wages	73.2	100.0	69.5	45.4	40.7	74.2
Employer contributions to a pension/ retirement fund	70.2	69.5	100.0	45.4	38.0	74.1
Paid leave	47.5	45.4	45.4	100.0	3499.0	50.0
Medical benefits	43.4	40.7	38.0	35.0	100.0	48.2
Overall	90.7	74.2	74.1	50.0	48.2	100.0

Source: 2014 Sierra Leone Labor Force Survey.

four times more likely than workers with no education to be in formal wage employment. Workers with tertiary educational attainment are nine times more likely than workers with no education to be employed in registered household enterprises. Formal wage employment and employment in registered household enterprises are more common in urban areas than in rural

Figure 4.1 Formality, by Characteristics of Individuals

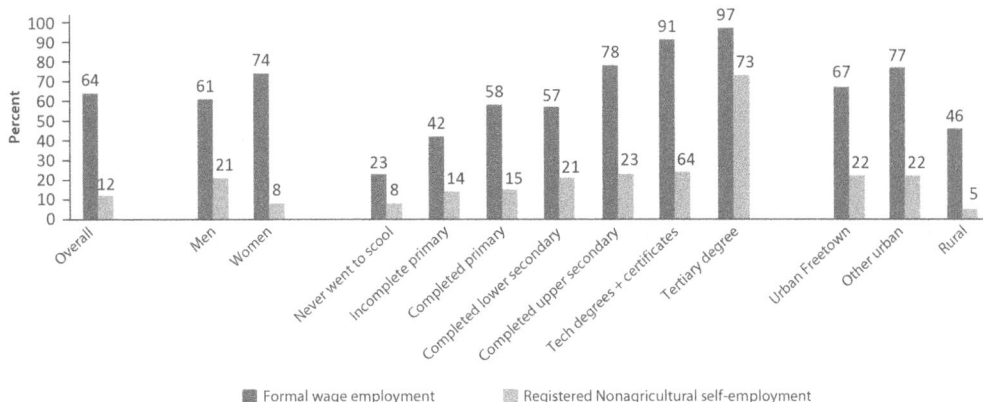

Source: 2014 Sierra Leone Labor Force Survey.

areas. Urban residents are more than four times more likely than rural residents to be employed in registered nonfarm household enterprises (22 percent vs. 5 percent). Not only is wage work rare in rural areas, but only 46 percent of all rural wage jobs are formal, whereas 67 percent of wage jobs in urban Freetown and 77 percent of wage jobs in other urban areas are formal. Formality among workers increases with age. The share of formal employment among wage employees peaks at over 86 percent among the 55–59 age group, while the peak in formality in nonagricultural self-employment occurs among the 45–49 age group (figure 4.2).

Individuals working in formal household enterprises are more likely than workers in informal household enterprises to face credit constraints. Of the workers in registered household enterprises, 53 percent face credit constraints, while 44 percent of workers in unregistered household enterprises face such constraints. This difference may be related to the fact that, among household enterprises involved in nonagricultural self-employment, formal enterprises rely less frequently than informal enterprises on family and friends as sources of borrowing (53 percent vs. 62 percent), while relying on microfinance institutions more frequently (16 percent vs. 8 percent). Formal sector nonagricultural employers depend on more well-established sources of credit, which may be more difficult to access than money from friends and family; the credit constraint may be exacerbated if formal enterprises need larger amounts of money than informal enterprises.

Statistical analysis indicates that some types of workers are, indeed, less likely to be able to obtain formal wage jobs.[3] The likelihood of working in a formal job, whether in wage employment or nonagricultural self-employment, is greater among men than women and increases with educational attainment. Formal jobs are more prevalent in Freetown and other urban areas, and the likelihood of obtaining a formal job roughly rises with age. Formal wage jobs are significantly

Figure 4.2 Formality, by Age Group

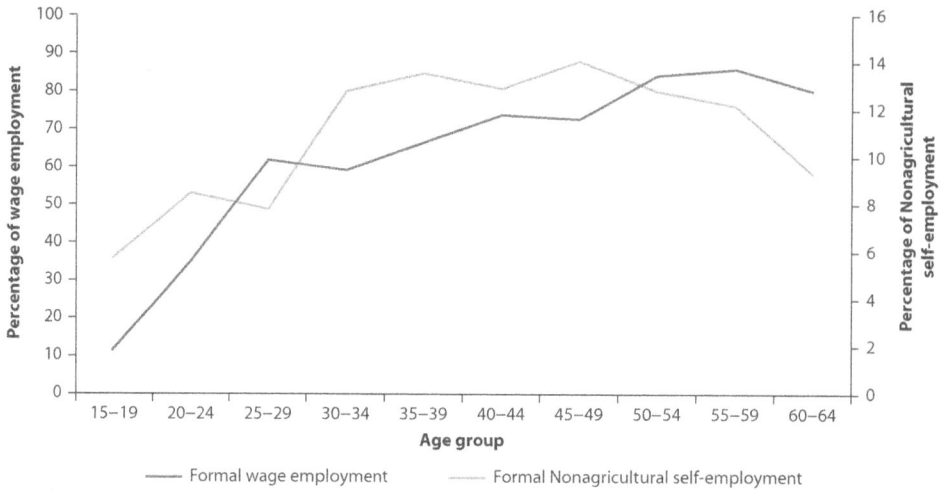

Source: 2014 Sierra Leone Labor Force Survey.

more common in services than in other sectors. Wage jobs in agriculture are almost never formal, while the self-employed are most likely to be registered in the mining sector and least likely to be registered in the construction sector.

Notes

1. Wage workers are considered part of the formal economy if any of the following is true: they have written contracts; income taxes are deducted from their wages; or their employers contribute to pension or retirement funds, paid leave, or medical benefits on their behalf. The nonagricultural self-employed are considered part of the formal economy if their household enterprises are registered with the Office of the Administrator and Registrar General, the National Revenue Authority, the National Social Security Insurance Trust, a Local City Council or Local District Council, or any other official formal entity.

2. By comparison, in nonagricultural self-employment, the self-employed who formally register their enterprises have an average of 9.0 years of education versus 8.3 years among the self-employed who do not register their enterprises.

3. This analysis is based on a probit model of formality, corrected for selection into employment. See appendix B.

CHAPTER 5

Youth

Youth (ages 15–35) represent the largest share of the overall population (66 percent) and more than half of the employed population (56 percent). Given the importance of youth in the population and in the labor market, this section explores the characteristics of education, employment outcomes, and other factors that could affect labor market outcomes among youth (photo 5.1). It first addresses basic education and then vocational training and apprenticeships among youth. An analysis of the transition from school to work follows, and then the main labor market outcomes are examined. The section concludes with a focus on the role of conflict and teenage pregnancy among youth.

Basic Education

Literacy rates are higher among youth than among older people (figure 5.1). Among young people, 51.8 percent report they can read and write (and are therefore literate), compared with 22 percent among older people (the 36–64 age group) and 41.7 percent among the working-age population. Men are more likely than women to be literate, and this differential is also present among youth (see chapter 2). Young men are more than two times more likely than older men to be literate, while young women are three times more likely than older women to be literate. As with the full population, the differences in literacy rates between urban and rural areas persist, though youth show higher literacy rates in all settings.

The youth population is more well educated than older people and the working-age population. Youth consists mainly of individuals who have never attended school (44.7 percent), while the corresponding shares among older people (36–64 age group) and the working-age population are, respectively, 75.5 percent and 55.2 percent (figure 5.2). However, youth include a higher share of individuals who have completed any level of education except technical degrees or certificates and tertiary degrees. Tertiary degrees are slightly

Photo 5.1   A young Okada (motorcycle taxi) rider in Western Urban looking out for his next client

Photo Credit: Andrea Martin.

Figure 5.1   Literacy, Youth (15–35) vs. Older People (36–64)

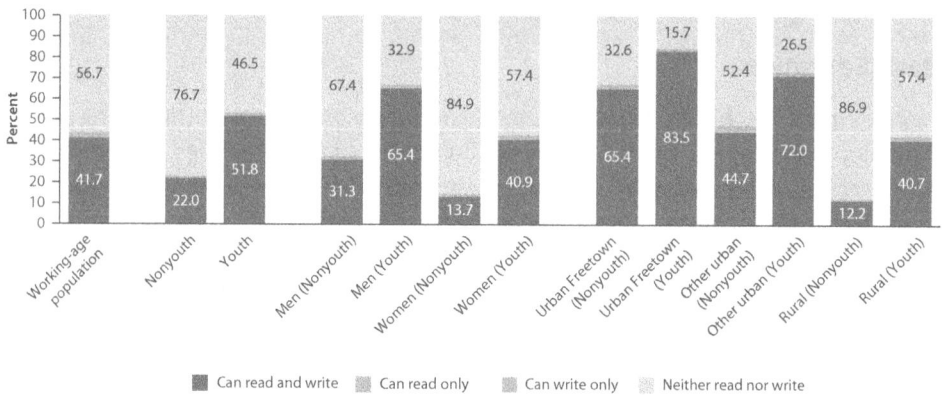

Note: Youth = individual ages 15–35; Nonyouth = individuals ages 36–64
Source: 2014 Sierra Leone Labor Force Survey.

underrepresented among youth; less than 0.5 percent of youth have tertiary degrees (vs. 1.0 percent among older people), and 1.2 percent have technical degrees or certificates (vs. 2.5 percent among older people). This underrepresentation of individuals with higher degrees derives partly from the fact that many young people in our sample are still in school and have not yet had the opportunity to obtain technical degrees, technical certificates, or tertiary degrees.

Figure 5.2 Education, Working-Age Population vs. Youth

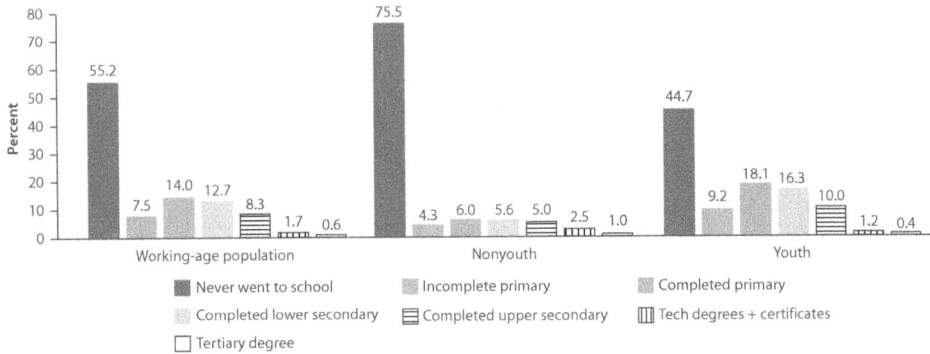

Note: Youth = individual ages 15–35; Nonyouth = individuals ages 36–64.

Source: 2014 Sierra Leone Labor Force Survey.

Years of education among youth subgroups mimic the education levels among the overall working-age population (figure 5.3). Overall, young people have slightly fewer years of education than the working-age population (an average of 8.6 years vs. 8.7 years) and around 0.7 fewer years of education than older people. However, this does not take into account the fact that many young people have not yet finished their schooling. Across subgroups, according to place of residence and migration status, the average years of education among youth show differences of more than a year of education, which mimics our findings among the total working-age population. The most striking difference in average years of education is between urban and rural areas. Youth in urban Freetown have almost 3.0 years of education more than youth in rural areas. Because tertiary education graduates tend to be concentrated in urban areas, this difference likely reflects an underestimate that will emerge when the youth currently in school finish their studies. There are also gender differences in average years of education, though they are not as large: young women have an average of around seven months less education than young men. Young migrants have more years of education (9.7) than young nonmigrants (8.4 years). Of all young migrants, 71 percent live in urban areas, and, given that a large share of migration is for purposes of education (see subsection 1.4), this gap will widen when youth complete their schooling. Among all subgroups, older people (the 36–64 age group) have more average years of education than youth (the 15–35 age group), though young people have not yet finished their studies.

The skill composition among youth varies across districts and provinces, but the clear leader in average years of education is the Western Area. With close to 2.0 fewer years of education, it is followed by Eastern Province (8.3 years), Southern Province (8.2 years), and Northern Province (8.1 years). Across districts, there is a large variation in average years of education among youth. The most highly educated district (the Western Area Urban District) averages 3.4 more years of education than the least well-educated district (Pujehun). The districts with the most well-educated working-age youth are the Western Area Urban District (10.1 years), the Western Area Rural District (9.5 years), and Bo

Figure 5.3 Years of Education among Youth, by Characteristics of Individuals

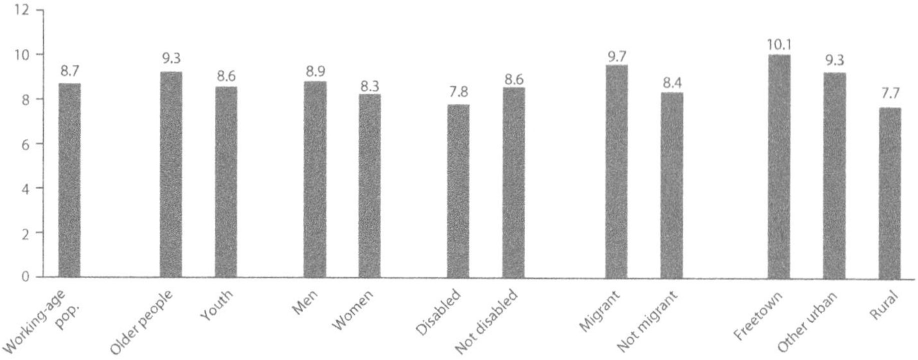

Source: 2014 Sierra Leone Labor Force Survey.

Map 5.1   Average Years of Education among Youth, by District

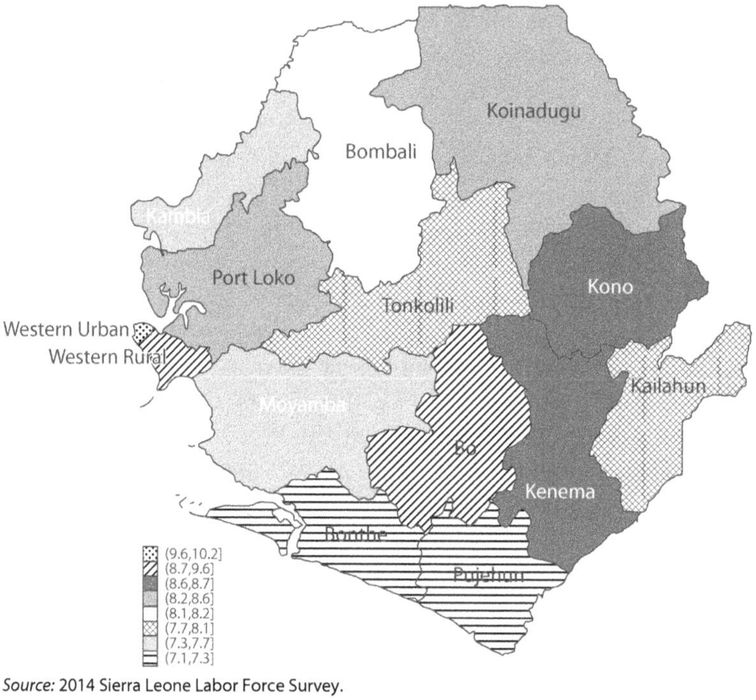

Source: 2014 Sierra Leone Labor Force Survey.

District (9.0 years) (map 5.1). The districts with the least well-educated youth are Pujehun (6.7 years), Bonthe (7.1 years), and Moyamba (7.5 years).

Around the world, the average years of education tend to increase with age up until a certain age; in Sierra Leone, this does not appear to be the case. There is an important increase in years of education from age 15 (an average of 6.5 years of education) to age 24 (an average of 10.1 years), for a total rise of

Figure 5.4 Average Years of Education, by Age

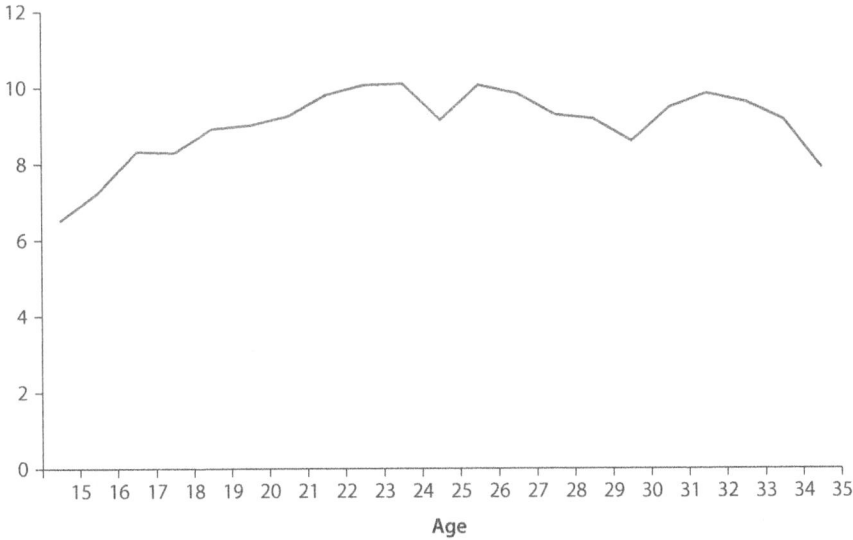

Source: 2014 Sierra Leone Labor Force Survey.

Figure 5.5 Share of Each 5-Year Age Group in School, by Gender

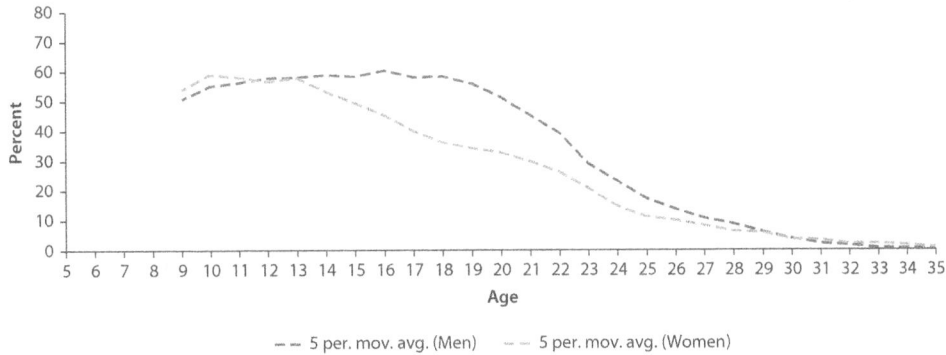

— — 5 per. mov. avg. (Men)   — — 5 per. mov. avg. (Women)

Source: 2014 Sierra Leone Labor Force Survey.

3.6 years of education (figure 5.4). The average number of years of education among youth fluctuates after age 24, ending at 7.9 average years of education among 35-year-olds. This drop in average years among older age groups of youth implies a trend among younger cohorts to stay in school longer, although the older age groups among youth were of school age during the war (a 35-year-old in 2014 was a 12-year-old at the onset of the war in 1991), and it is likely their education was affected by the conflict (see section "Conflict").

Boys leave school at different ages than girls. Although boys and girls have roughly similar rates of school attendance up to age 12, girls start to leave school much sooner, and the share of girls in school declines after age 13 (figure 5.5).

Findings from the 2014 Labor Force Survey in Sierra Leone
http://dx.doi.org/10.1596/978-1-4648-0742-8

Boys stay in school longer and only start leaving en masse around age 19. As a result, once in the labor force, men can be expected to have more education than women (see chapter 2)

Vocational Training and Apprenticeships

Only 5 percent of youth have participated in vocational training, which is similar to the share among the overall working-age population (figure 5.6). As with the full population, there are noticeable differences in terms of gender and place of residence among youth who have some vocational training: 7 percent of men compared with 4 percent of women have undergone vocational training, while 11 percent of youth in urban Freetown have undergone training compared with 3 percent of youth in rural areas. Because vocational training is often started at younger ages and is concentrated among people who have never attended school (see chapter 2), measures of the incidence and length of training are less likely to be subject to the incomplete spell issues that affect the education measures discussed in section "Basic Education".

Among youth who have undertaken vocational training, the average number of years spent in training is 2.1 years (figure 5.7). Unlike the case of average years of education, rural youth have undergone more average years of vocational training than urban youth (2.3 years vs. 1.9 years). Young women receive an average of 0.5 fewer years of training than young men, who average 2.3 years of training. The average duration of training is shorter among migrants and the disabled than among nonmigrants and the nondisabled, but migrants are more than twice as likely as nonmigrants to have received some training.

All these results are similar to what is observed among the overall population, with the exception of the disabled (see chapter 2). Although nondisabled youth who have undergone training spend a similar amount of time in training as the general working-age population (2.1 years vs. 2.2 years), disabled youth spend

Figure 5.6 Share of Youth Who Have Received Vocational Training, by Characteristics of Individuals

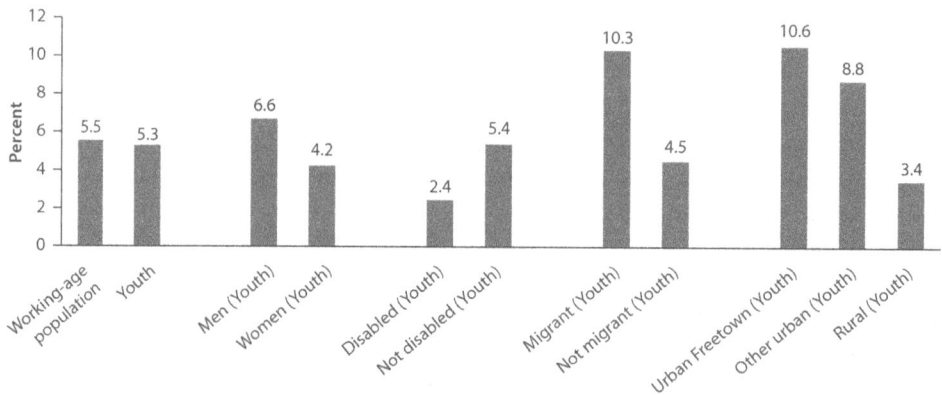

Source: 2014 Sierra Leone Labor Force Survey.

Figure 5.7 Average Years of Training among Youth, by Characteristics of Individuals

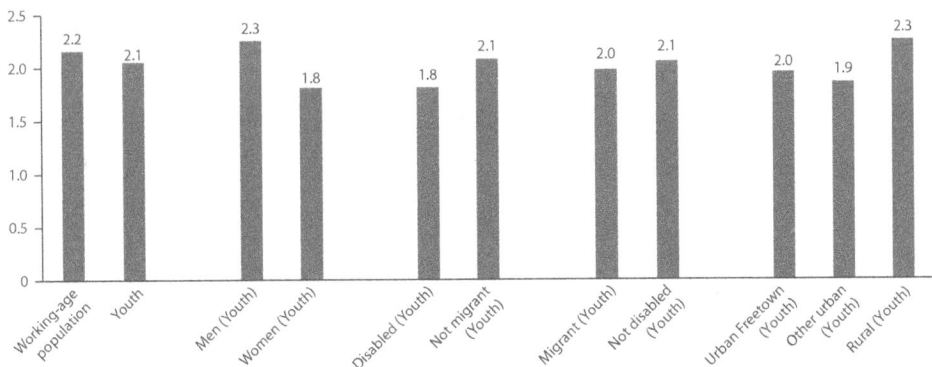

Source: 2014 Sierra Leone Labor Force Survey.

an average of 7.2 fewer months in training when they participate in training than the disabled in the entire working-age population (1.8 years vs. 2.4 years), indicating that disabled workers who are not among the youth population have a much longer average duration in training when they have participated. Part of the extra training among older disabled workers may be related to programs among decommissioned soldiers and other disabled individuals in the immediate aftermath of the conflict, and these programs may no longer be available among disabled youth.

Geographically, there are large differences. Pujehun District shows the highest average years of vocational training among youth (figure 5.8). The Western Area has the highest incidence of training among youth (10.2 percent), but the average duration of training there is the shortest, though it is essentially the same number of years as in Southern and Northern provinces. Because the Western Area also has the highest level of education, this may indicate that, in areas with low formal education, individuals, in some cases, substitute formal education for a longer duration in vocational training.

Young people with no certified formal education (no schooling or only incomplete primary) tend to undergo vocational training for more years than people with at least some certified formal education. This is an example of longer training spells substituting for missing education. Training among youth with no education lasts an average of 2.4 years, roughly the same duration as among youth with incomplete primary education, while youth who have completed upper-secondary school receive an average of around 1.7 years of training (figure 5.9).

The average number of years of training required among youth to obtain various certifications varies between 1.8 years and 2.8 years (see figure 5.9).[1] Youth who obtain nursing diplomas spend an average of 2.8 years in training. Receiving city and guilds certifications require an average of 1.8 years of training. Relative to the overall working-age population, youth spend fewer years in training to obtain agricultural trade certifications (2.0 years vs. 2.4 years). Part of

Figure 5.8 Average Years of Training among Youth, by Province and District

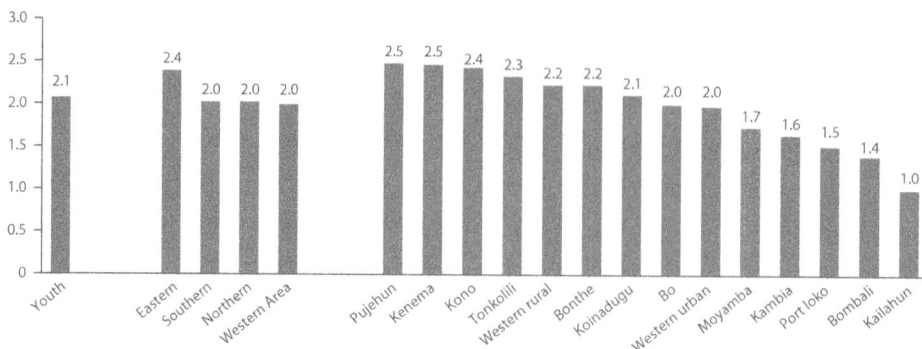

Source: 2014 Sierra Leone Labor Force Survey.

Figure 5.9 Years of Training, by Educational Attainment and Professional Certification

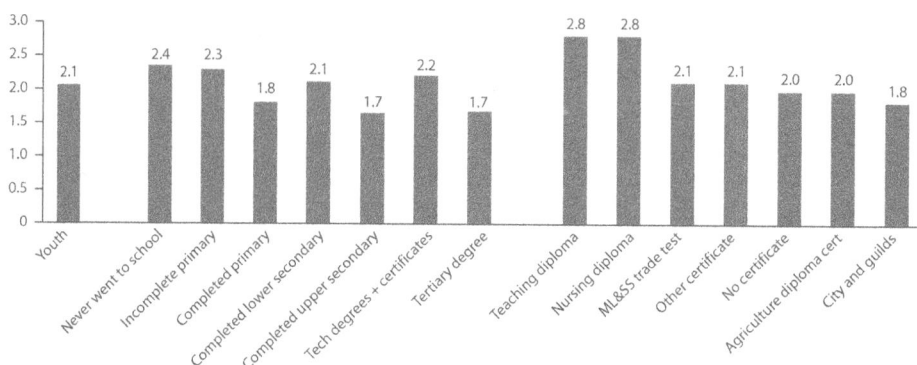

Source: 2014 Sierra Leone Labor Force Survey.

the difference may be explained by youth who have not yet completed all their vocational training. However, a more likely explanation is that opportunities for obtaining training certifications have increased over time, and shorter programs may have been introduced that were unavailable to older cohorts; however, sufficient data on training are not available to examine this issue.

Youth who participate in vocational training have more years of formal education than youth who serve in apprenticeships. Youth who participate in vocational training have an average of 9.5 years of formal education compared with 8.6 years among youth who serve as apprentices (figure 5.10). This mainly reflects the fact that relatively more youth who serve in apprenticeships have never attended school. Completion of lower- or upper-secondary school is far more common than technical degrees and certificates and tertiary degrees among the youth who undergo training.

Only 6 percent of youth have ever served apprenticeships, and, similar to the working-age population, there are key differences depending on gender and location of residence (figure 5.11). Thus, 11 percent of young men have been apprentices,

Figure 5.10 Vocational Training and Apprenticeships, by Formal Educational Attainment

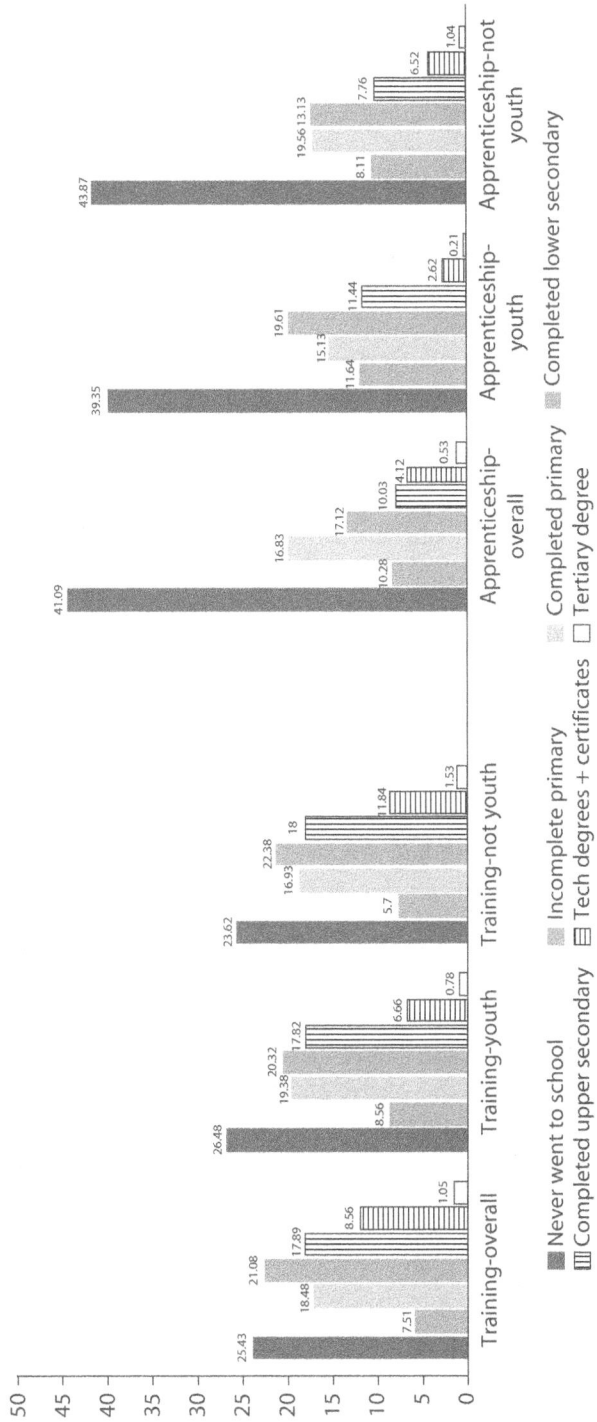

Legend:
- Never went to school
- Completed upper secondary
- Incomplete primary
- Tech degrees + certificates
- Completed primary
- Tertiary degree
- Completed lower secondary

Training-overall: 25.43, 7.51, 18.48, 21.08, 17.89, 8.56, 1.05

Training-youth: 26.48, 8.56, 19.38, 20.32, 17.82, 6.66, 0.78

Training-not youth: 23.62, 5.7, 16.93, 22.38, 18, 11.84, 1.53

Apprenticeship-overall: 41.09, 10.28, 16.83, 17.12, 10.03, 4.12, 0.53

Apprenticeship-youth: 39.35, 11.64, 15.13, 19.61, 11.44, 2.62, 0.21

Apprenticeship-not youth: 43.87, 8.11, 19.56, 13.13, 7.76, 6.52, 1.04

Source: 2014 Sierra Leone Labor Force Survey.

Figure 5.11 Frequency of Apprenticeships among Youth, by Characteristics of Individuals

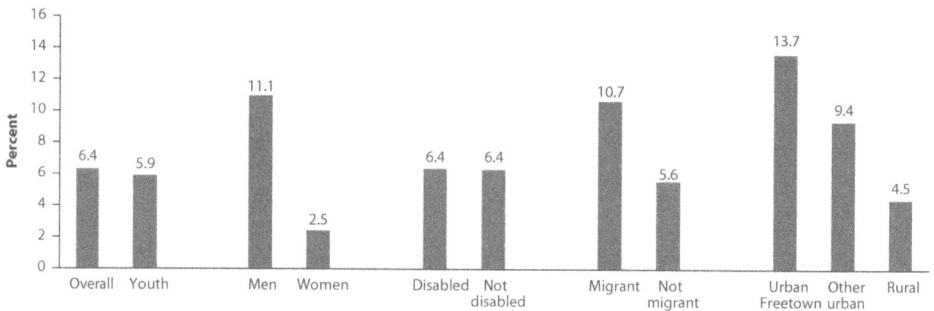

Source: 2014 Sierra Leone Labor Force Survey.

compared with 2 percent of young women, which are slightly lower than the corresponding figures for the overall working-age population (11.1 percent for men and 2.5 percent for women). Among young residents of urban Freetown, 11 percent have served as apprentices, compared with 4 percent among young rural residents.

Few youth reported they had benefited from employment programs in the previous 12 months. Among youth, 1.9 percent reported they had directly benefited in the previous 12 months from employment-related social protection programs run by the government, donors, or NGOs. The program youth most commonly reported that they benefited from is the Smallholder Commercialization Program (42 percent). No noticeable differences across gender or location of residence show up in the responses on this issue.

The Transition from School to Work

There are several key points along the path of youth through formal schooling at which young people exit education for work, but the main point of the transition begins around age 17. Roughly 50 percent of each school-age cohort is still in school between ages 8 and 14. The share of each age cohort still in school drops by a quarter between ages 14 and 15, thereby reaching 38 percent among 15-year-olds (figure 5.12). Another major wave of exits occurs between ages 17 and 18. The share still in school thus falls from 38 percent to 35 percent among the 17–18 age group. The next wave of exits takes place between ages 19 and 20, and the share of this age group still in school drops from 34 percent to 18 percent.

The vast majority of youth who leave school begin to work, including women. Girls tend to leave school at slightly earlier ages than boys (see figure 5.5). However, as the share of girls in school falls, the share of girls in employment increases by roughly the same amount, while the only discernible peak in labor force withdrawal among women occurs when they are in their mid-20s (figure 5.13). Similar results are apparent among boys, although the peak in labor force withdrawal among young men occurs when they are in their late 20s (figure 5.14).

Figure 5.12 The Transition from School to Work

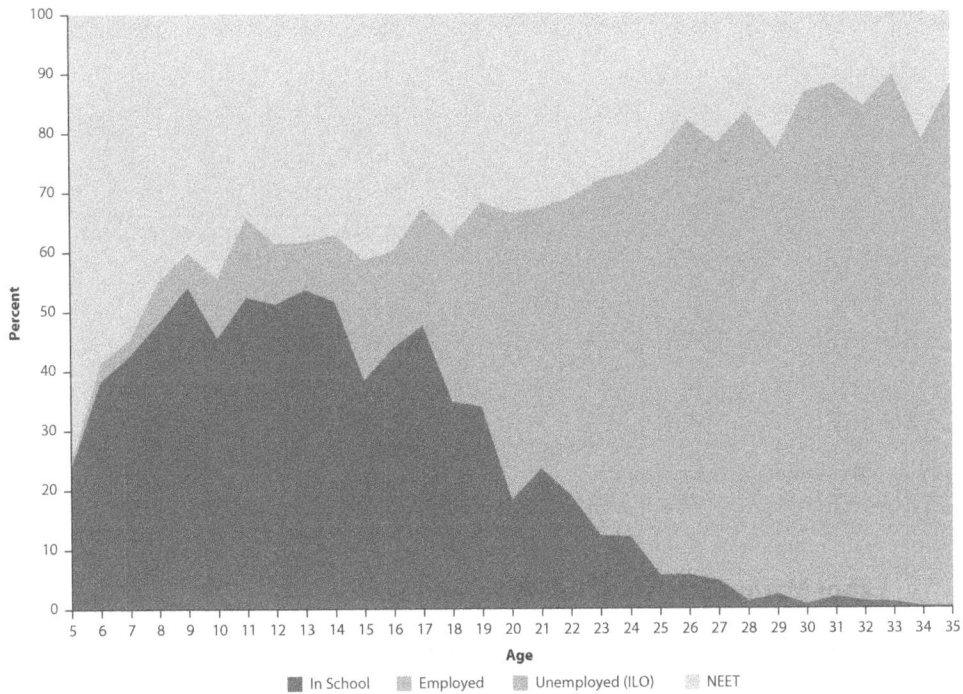

Source: 2014 Sierra Leone Labor Force Survey.

Figure 5.13 Transitions across Labor Market Status, Young Women, 5-Year Moving Average

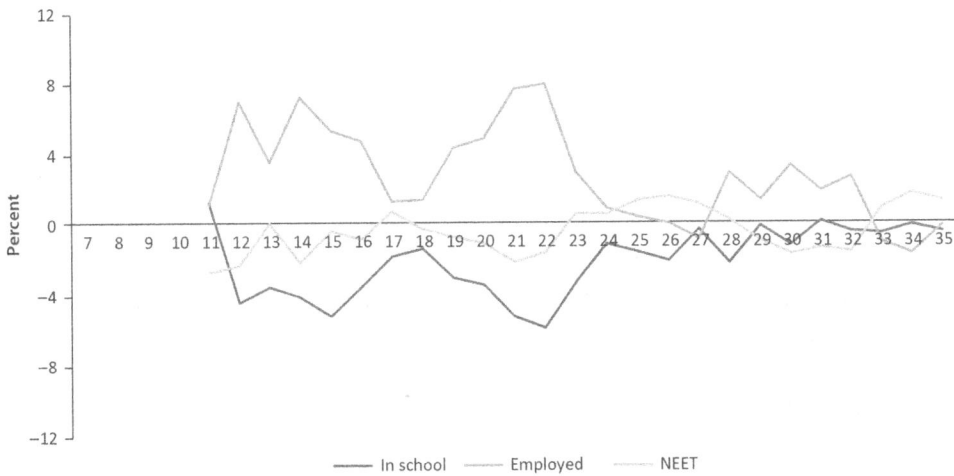

Source: 2014 Sierra Leone Labor Force Survey.

Findings from the 2014 Labor Force Survey in Sierra Leone
http://dx.doi.org/10.1596/978-1-4648-0742-8

Figure 5.14 Transitions across Labor Market Status, Young Men, 5-Year Moving Average

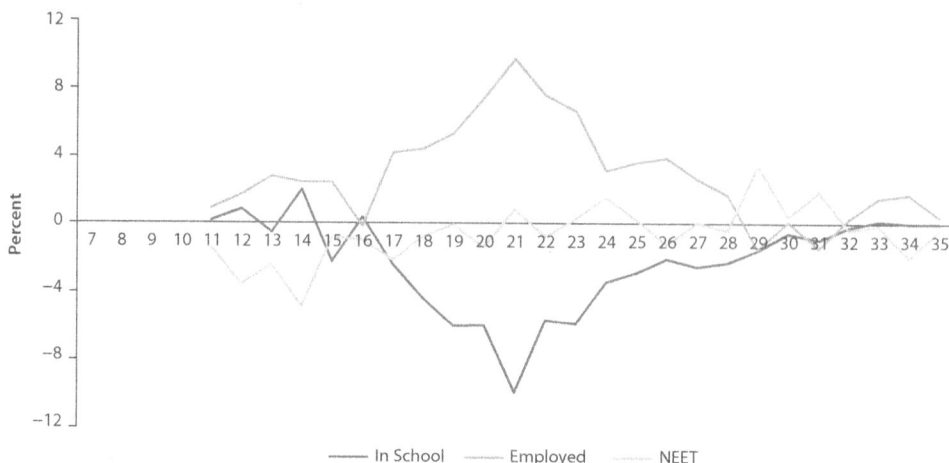

In School — Employed — NEET

Source: 2014 Sierra Leone Labor Force Survey.

Labor Market Statistics, Job Type, and Sector

Youth (15–35) participate less in the labor market and fare worse in terms of employment and unemployment compared with older people (36–64). Relative to older people, the share of employed youth is much smaller (81.3 percent vs. 52.4 percent) (table 5.1). There is a 25 percentage point difference in labor force participation between young men and older men in these age groups (53.4 percent vs. 88.2 percent) and a 20 percentage point difference between young women and older women (57.6 percent vs. 78.6 percent). A significant portion of this difference arises because many youth are still in school and not simultaneously working. The unemployment rate is also higher among youth than among older people (5.9 percent vs. 2.2 percent). The highest unemployment rate (ILO) among young men occurs among youth in urban Freetown (14.0 percent), while the highest overall unemployment rate (ILO) by gender or by broad age group (ages 15–35 or 35–64) occurs among young men (7.7 percent).

The differences in the type of job and sector of employment are not large between youth (15–35) and older people (36–64). Unpaid work accounts for a more substantial share of youth than older people, especially in urban Freetown, where the respective shares are 4.7 percent and 0.0 percent (figure 5.15). Young women are less likely than older women to be employed in services (37 percent vs. 42 percent) (figure 5.16). In general, the trends in employment by job type and sector seem to follow the same pattern among youth and the overall working-age population.

Table 5.1 Key Aggregate Labor Market Statistics, Youth (15–35) vs. Older People (36–64)

	Working-age population (%)	Nonyouth (%)	Youth (%)	Men (nonyouth) (%)	Men (youth) (%)	Women (nonyouth) (%)	Women (youth) (%)	Urban Freetown (non-youth) (%)	Urban Freetown (youth) (%)	Other urban (nonyouth) (%)	Other urban (youth) (%)	Rural (nonyouth) (%)	Rural (youth) (%)
Employed	62.20	81.30	52.40	86.50	49.30	76.70	55.00	77.00	36.70	79.50	38.50	82.20	59.00
Workforce (ILO)	65.00	83.10	55.70	88.20	53.40	78.60	57.60	83.10	42.60	82.20	42.50	83.30	61.60
Unemployed (ILO)	2.80	1.80	3.30	1.70	4.10	2.00	2.60	6.10	5.90	2.80	4.00	1.10	2.60
Broad unemployed	9.10	7.10	10.10	6.70	9.30	7.50	10.70	10.20	12.80	6.10	8.70	7.00	10.00
Unemployment rate (ILO)	4.30	2.20	5.90	1.90	7.70	2.50	4.50	7.30	14.00	3.40	9.40	1.40	4.20

Source: 2014 Sierra Leone Labor Force Survey.

Figure 5.15 Main Job Type among Youth (15–35), by Gender and Location

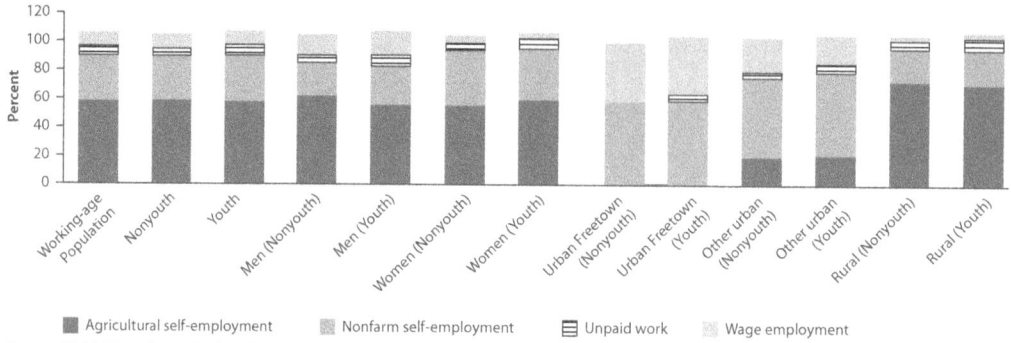

Source: 2014 Sierra Leone Labor Force Survey.

Figure 5.16 Sector of Main Employment among Youth (15–35), by Gender and Location

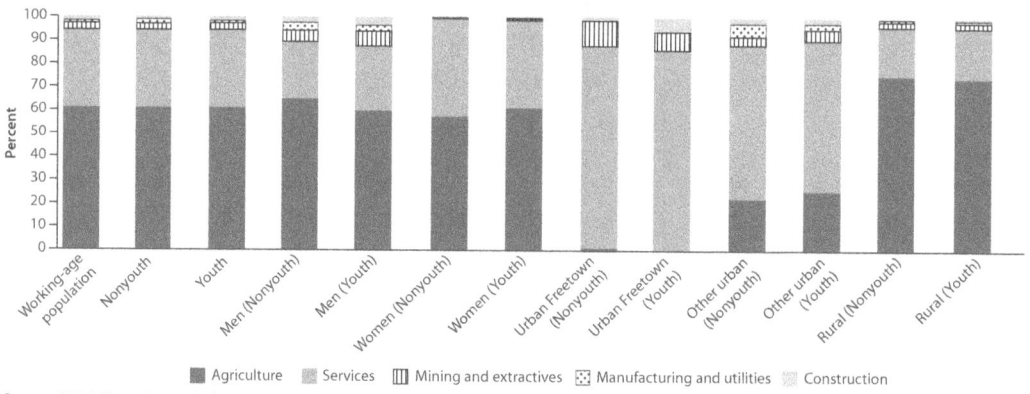

Source: 2014 Sierra Leone Labor Force Survey.

Conflict

Youth (ages 15–35) claim to have been less affected by conflict than older people (36–64). Among older people, 78.0 percent declare they suffered severe loss or destruction of assets because of conflict, while 41.3 percent of youth declare they suffered severe loss (figure 5.17). Only 5.1 percent of the older cohorts say they were not severely affected by the conflict, while the corresponding share is six times larger among youth (31.6 percent). An important segment of youth was among the school-age population during the war, and the conflict likely had important effects on their education.[2] These results are compatible with the results associated with our consideration of the reasons for migration (see figure 1.23) and suggest that, while youth were severely affected by the conflict, the effects were less direct than the mere destruction of property. Thus, employment policies centered on conflict-related interventions need to be attentive to the type of support provided because most of the benefits supplied by programs designed to replace lost physical assets are likely to be diverted from

Figure 5.17 The Population Effects of the Civil (Rebel) War, 1991–2002, Youth vs. Older People

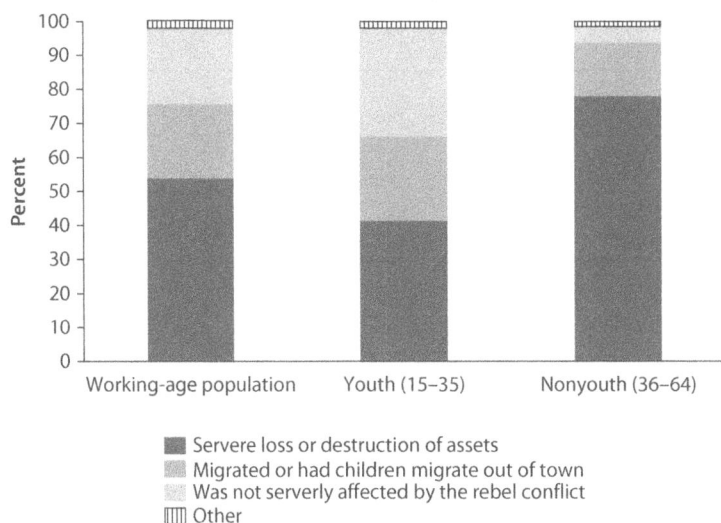

Legend:
- Servere loss or destruction of assets
- Migrated or had children migrate out of town
- Was not serverly affected by the rebel conflict
- Other

Source: 2014 Sierra Leone Labor Force Survey.

youth, and other skills-based policy interventions aimed at improving labor market outcomes that more carefully target youth should be considered.

Teenage Pregnancy

Among women between the ages of 15 and 35 (young women), 66.5 percent had their first child between the ages of 15 and 19. Teenage pregnancy is a concern not only because of the potential negative effects on the children but also because of the potential negative effects on the labor market outcomes among the mothers. Having a child when they are still in basic education increases the chances that they will quit school and makes reentering school more difficult, negatively affecting labor market outcomes. As seen in table 5.2, working-age women who were teen mothers have 7.8 years of education, compared with the 8.9 years among working-age women who were not teen mothers. The earnings of women who were not teen mothers are also higher than the earnings of women who were teen mothers (Le 730,000 vs. Le 560,000). Having a child while still a teenager also affects the type of job a woman may obtain. Among women who were not teen mothers, 6.6 percent are wage employed, while only 2.8 percent are wage employed among the women who were teen mothers. Conversely, the share of women working in agricultural self-employment is 6.4 percentage points higher among those who were teen mothers relative to those who were not. Most of the differences in earnings and job type disappear once controls are implemented for education level, suggesting that education is the main channel through which teenage pregnancy influences labor market outcomes.

Findings from the 2014 Labor Force Survey in Sierra Leone
http://dx.doi.org/10.1596/978-1-4648-0742-8

Table 5.2 Women Who Were Teen Mothers vs. Women Who Were Not Teen Mothers

	Working age women	Wasn't a teenage mother	Was a teenage mother
Years of education	8.4	8.9	7.8
Median earnings	618,000	730,000	560,000
Wage employment	4.5%	6.6%	2.8%
Agricultural self-employment	58.7%	54.2%	60.6%
Nonagricultural self-employment	36.8%	39.1%	36.6%

Source: 2014 Sierra Leone Labor Force Survey.

Notes

1. The number of observations among the subgroups of youth is small; so, the data should be interpreted with caution. For example, among the subgroup representing tertiary education, there are only six observations. For the certificates for nursing, teaching, agricultural trades, city workers, and trade guilds, there is an average of 23 observations.

2. People who were 37 years old when the sample was surveyed (2014) were 14 years old at the onset of the war in 1991 and were thus too young to be included among the working-age population. Likewise, people aged 17 at the time of the sample were 5 years old in 2002 and are thus not expected to have started school before the conflict had ended. Because people who were of school age during the conflict were 18–37 years old when the sample was taken, it is impossible to assign differences in the distribution of education among this age group relative to the older age group to the effects of the conflict.

CHAPTER 6

Summary and Policy Recommendations

This report summarizes the results of Sierra Leone's 2014 Labor Force Survey and suggests five important dimensions of the economy that merit further attention. The Overview presents basic descriptive statistics and detailed breakdowns of the structure of employment and earnings in Sierra Leone (photo 6.1). It raises issues that are explored in sections on skills (chapter 2), farming and non-farm household enterprises (chapter 3), informality (chapter 4), and youth (chapter 5). The results observed in Sierra Leone are fairly typical of the results in countries at a similar stage of development.

The first key dimension is the importance of agriculture for the labor market. Agricultural self-employment accounts for 59 percent of all jobs, and the agricultural sector, including paid agricultural workers, represents nearly 61 percent of all jobs. The average pay in agriculture is, however, the lowest across all sectors of employment, and the workers in the sector are the least skilled, which reflects the sector's low productivity. Moreover, a large share of agricultural workers live in households that face credit constraints or do not have access to extension services. Policies to improve the productivity of agriculture are thus likely to have a substantial impact because they would address the lowest baseline and cover the most people, but they would also need to be adapted to meet the constraints faced by farming households.

After agriculture, the service sector provides the most jobs; well-paying sectors such as mining and extractive industries are only minor contributors to the labor market. The service sector is relatively well paid, and it employs far more of the most skilled workers than any other sector. Because services provide wage employment (unlike agriculture, in which wage employment is negligible), policies to encourage the growth of service firms, in particular by hiring wage workers, could lead to greater overall productivity in the economy.

The second key dimension is the small share of workers who earn wages: wage employment is primarily reserved to the public sector and to the most well-educated people in the workforce. The limited share of wage employment

**Photo 6.1   A young mother in Koinadugu Town heads home
after a literacy class**

Photo Credit: Andrea Martin.

is a potential source of concern in policy making because any labor market
regulations or policies that affect wage workers or, more specifically, formal
sector wage workers are likely to have only a limited impact because of the
restrained coverage of formal wage jobs. Moreover, because most of these jobs
are in the public sector, legislation is not necessary to implement change in
favor of these workers. Policy interventions to encourage the growth of wage
employment, such as training in business practices and improving the business
environment to encourage business growth among self-employed entrepreneurs, could be a focus of efforts to shift the balance of employment toward
wage work.

Findings from the 2014 Labor Force Survey in Sierra Leone
http://dx.doi.org/10.1596/978-1-4648-0742-8

The weak presence of wage work is counterbalanced by the dominance of self-employment. Because self-employment is the norm among those individuals who might potentially work, unemployed workers do not focus their attention on wage jobs, but, rather, on starting their own businesses. The importance of the capital constraints affecting the unemployed suggests that, more than active labor market programs that attempt to place the unemployed in wage jobs, policies designed to improve the access to credit and finance could have a greater impact in boosting employment.

The third key dimension is the disparity between outcomes across educational attainment and gender. Employment rates are similar among men and women, who, however, occupy different sorts of jobs if they obtain employment and have different skills. Although employment rates are highest at both ends of the education spectrum, there are far more graduates of tertiary education who are among the (ILO) unemployed relative to individuals who have never attended school. If they work, the least well educated are found almost exclusively in agriculture, while few graduates of tertiary education are active in agriculture. By contrast, the public sector, NGOs, and international organizations tend to be the most frequent sources of jobs among graduates of tertiary schools and individuals with technical degrees or certificates. This is potentially problematic—in particular, given the small wage sector—if the most educated spend their time waiting (in unemployment) for public sector jobs rather than starting their own enterprises.

Outcomes also differ among youth and older adults. Young people are much less likely to be employed, especially young men, although their situation is improving relative to older individuals. The literacy rate among young people is more than double the rates among older adults, and youth are generally more well educated. That girls leave school earlier than boys is the main reason behind gender differences in skills, though most young people who leave school move into employment; leaving school to remain out of the labor force or enter unemployment is rare. Young women who have children before age 20, however, are especially penalized on the labor market. Teen mothers earn three-quarters of the earnings of older mothers, have nearly a 60 percent lower chance of obtaining wage jobs and are 12 percent more likely to be self-employed in agriculture, the least productive and least well-paying sector.

The fourth key dimension is the geographical heterogeneity of labor market outcomes and, particularly, the rural–urban divide. Labor markets are clearly different in rural and urban areas. Rural labor markets rely more heavily on agriculture and self-employment, attract fewer migrants, and depend on a less well-skilled workforce. The opposite is true among urban areas and districts such as the Western Area Urban District. This implies that policy initiatives need to be geographically targeted and sensitive to the specificities of local labor markets. Policies to improve productivity in rural areas will need to focus on agriculture and cannot assume a high initial skill level or even a high literacy rate among participants, whereas policies targeted at urban areas can focus on services and provide higher-level training and assistance.

Findings from the 2014 Labor Force Survey in Sierra Leone
http://dx.doi.org/10.1596/978-1-4648-0742-8

Finally, the first priority among poverty reduction initiatives should be to increase labor force participation and employment. The findings of this report suggest that labor force participation and employment are closely linked to poverty outcomes, while issues such as skills, labor legislation, or the industrial structure of the country, although important, are less closely connected to poverty outcomes. Ideally, additional employment should be created in higher-productivity areas, and investment and skills development should aim at more employment and more highly productive jobs. Nonetheless, the largest initial constraint on employment appears to be access to capital; so, policies to improve formal or informal financial markets have the greatest potential to reduce poverty. These policies could target specific groups that are disproportionately likely to stay out of the labor market, such as the population segments that started school, but did not get past secondary education, to maximize the potential reduction in poverty.

Key Concepts in the 2014 Sierra Leone Labor Force Survey (SLLFS) Analysis

This appendix presents the key concepts used in the analysis of the 2014 Sierra Leone Labor Force Survey, which was collected between July and August 2014. It focuses on a subset of core indicators in the SLLFS data. The layout of this appendix is as follows. It first introduces a few general concepts that will be referenced throughout, discusses the level of disaggregation, and highlights the main subgroups covered in the data analysis. It then presents the definitions of core labor market indicators based on the latest ILO guidelines (see appendix C).[1] Finally, it describes the key indicators in the topics of the main analysis: key job types and sectors of employment, household agricultural activities, nonfarm household enterprises, links to the extractive sector, migration and civil conflict, and youth employment. SLLFS question numbers that correspond to the key concepts referenced are also documented.

Labor Force Survey–Related Concepts

Household members: the SLLFS recognizes as household members all individuals who usually live and eat together or, more precisely, who usually share shelter and eating arrangements.

SLLFS eligible: In Part I of the survey, potential respondents in surveyed households are considered SLLFS eligible if they are at least five years of age and spent at least four nights each week in the surveyed household during the previous four weeks. The sections of the survey instrument addressed to individuals require survey respondents to be SLLFS eligible, with the exception being the section on other activities and time use.

Working-age population: A well-defined working-age population is key in determining labor market indicators. The ILO does not have a specific recommendation on working age. In the SLLFS analysis, working age is between 15 and

64 years, following the definition of the economically active population in the World Bank World Development Indicators database. Unless otherwise specified, for instance, in the case of youth (ages 15–35), it is assumed the age range under analysis is within the working-age population.

As recommended by the ILO, the national system of statistics on employment should cover the labor activities of all age groups, including children on whom separate statistics are needed. Given that the SLLFS collects labor force statistics on individuals five years of age and above, information on children in employment is available in the SLLFS. Child labor, which is the engagement of children in prohibitive work, and, more generally, types of work slated for elimination are measured by the number or share of individuals who, during a specified period, were engaged in work under the worst conditions, employment below minimum age, or hazardous unpaid household services. However, information on working conditions is not collected in the SLLFS.

Reference period: In assembling data on current labor activities, all questions relate to a short reference period, the last full week (Monday to Sunday) preceding the date of the interview. For usual labor activities, a longer reference period of 12 months is used. Unless otherwise specified, the labor force indicators referenced in this report are based on the shorter reference period.

Levels of Disaggregation

In addition to the analysis of labor market indicators at the national level, the analysis is carried out across various dimensions, including breakdowns by district and province, the urban–rural divide, and gender. The analysis of relevant subpopulations takes place as needed. For instance, nonfarm household enterprise activities are predominantly an urban phenomenon, while agricultural activities occur primarily in rural areas. Important subgroups such as youth population are analyzed separately. Unless otherwise specified, the indicators referenced should be understood to cover the working-age population at the national level.

Key Traditional Labor Market Indicators

The employed: The employed population is defined as individuals who worked for at least one hour in the last full week previous to the interview (Monday to Sunday) to produce goods or provide services for pay or profit in nonfarm self-employment, wage employment, agricultural activities, or as paid apprentices. In addition, respondents who were temporarily absent from economic activities during the previous full week are also considered among the employed. This latter group includes individuals who were absent from work because of poor health, vacation, or maternity or paternity leave, individuals who were away from work for either less than a month or one to three months, or individuals otherwise still receiving pay, but not working. Individuals who only worked in own-use production, as unpaid trainees, as volunteers, or in nonproductive activities are not considered employed. The employment rate, or employment-to-population ratio, measures the proportion of the country's working-age population that is employed.

Unemployment: ILO unemployment is based on three criteria, namely, individuals who are (1) without employment, (2) currently available for work, or (3) seeking employment. Individuals are considered to be without employment if they did not work in the previous full week and have no economic activities to which to return. Currently available for work means that the individuals were available for work during the previous full week or are available to undertake work during the next two weeks if the opportunity arises. Seeking work is defined as looking for a job or trying to start one's own business. The unemployment rate is calculated as a percentage by dividing the number of unemployed individuals by the number of all individuals currently in the labor force (see the definition below). The unemployment rate alone does not completely portray the challenges in employment and in the labor market of a country. It is complemented by indicators of labor underutilization, such as time-related underemployment described below, to provide a complete picture of the labor market. Broader measures of underemployment are described below.

Time-related underemployment: The concept of time-related underemployment complements the unemployment rate by helping to measure the mismatch between labor supply and labor demand. In essence, it captures information on individuals who are currently working less than they would like. While there are different approaches to this measurement, a simple way to gauge time-related underemployment is to use the percentage of individuals who are working part time, but who wish to work more. This covers individuals who: (1) worked an average of less than 8 hours a day for five days during the previous full week, (2) expressed a willingness to work more, or (3) gave economic reasons for not working more hours (for example, lack of business activity, lack of finance).

Broader measures of underemployment cover the concepts recommended by a resolution adopted by the 19th International Conference of Labor Statisticians. This includes the combined rate of time-related underemployment and unemployment, the combined rate of unemployment and the potential labor force, or a composite measure of labor underutilization, the official definitions of which can be found in paragraph 73 in the resolution document (see appendix C). In addition, the ratio of the sum of the total unemployed and all discouraged workers to the sum of the labor force, plus all discouraged workers is also adopted as a broad unemployment rate that takes the discouraged job seekers into account. This is recommended as an alternative measure of labor underutilization by the U.S. Bureau of Labor Statistics.

Labor force participation: The labor force of a country includes both the employed and the unemployed. The labor force participation rate is the ratio between the labor force and the working-age population.

Inactivity: The inactive population includes individuals who are not in the labor force, that is, they are neither employed nor unemployed. The inactivity rate is the share of the working-age population that is not in the labor force.

Findings from the 2014 Labor Force Survey in Sierra Leone
http://dx.doi.org/10.1596/978-1-4648-0742-8

Figure A.1 Relationships among Key Labor Market Concepts

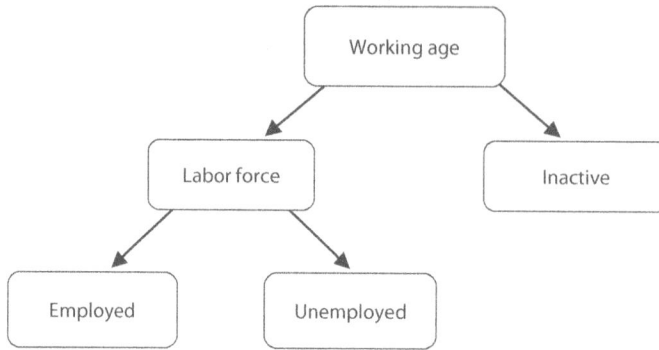

Source: 2014 Sierra Leone Labor Force Survey.

Discouraged job seekers: Discouraged job-seekers are individuals who want to work and are available to work, but did not seek employment for labor market–specific reasons such as failure to find a suitable job; lack of experience, qualifications, or jobs matching the skills of the individuals; and lack of jobs in the location; the individuals are considered too young or too old by prospective employers.

Figure A.1 summarizes the relationship between some of the key concepts presented above.

Formality of employment and nonfarm household enterprises: According to the ILO guidelines, informal employment represents the total number of informal jobs. Although closely linked, the formality of employment does not depend entirely on the formality of enterprises defined according to the availability of contracts and certain employment benefits. The World Bank's Silver Standard for labor force surveys has more specific definitions based on the ILO guidelines, according to which self-employment and family employment are informal. Paid employment is considered formal if it is associated with a pension scheme, a health insurance plan, or a contract, regardless of enterprise. Otherwise, the employment is informal. In the SLLFS, the main employment activity determines the formality of the employment. Also, according to the World Bank's Silver Standard, a nonfarm enterprise employing fewer than five individuals and unregistered enterprises are considered informal.

Indicators of Job Types and Main Sectors of Employment

This report considers three main types of current economic activity: wage and salary employment, self-employment (divided into nonagricultural self-employment and agricultural self-employment), and unpaid work.

These are determined according to employment status. Thus, regular, casual, or seasonal paid employees and paid apprentices are classified under wage and salary employment; the self-employed, whether or not they have regular employees, and members of producer cooperatives are classified under self-employment; and unpaid apprentices and unpaid help are classified under unpaid work. Furthermore, the International Standard Classification of Occupations codes for main goods and services provide information that helps distinguish agricultural and nonagricultural activities under the self-employed classification. Unpaid work and subsistence farming activities (a subgroup of the agricultural sector) are classified as general forms of work, but not as employment activities as outlined above.

Indicators of Household Agricultural Activities

On the agricultural sector, the SLLFS collected information on the crops, livestock, and landownership status of respondents. Basic analysis of principal crops includes the sum of households that grow each type of crop and the ratio between the number of households that grow the crop and the total number of households in the agricultural sector. A similar analysis can be carried out on livestock ownership. Information on landownership can be obtained directly from responses to the question on landownership and confirmed through the responses to the question about the possession of legal titles to dwellings. As part of the core agricultural indicators, the use of mechanical equipment and labor inputs by household members or others outside the household during the previous season are calculated as key agricultural inputs.

Indicators on Nonfarm Household Enterprises

Nonfarm household enterprises, which, in the context of Sierra Leone, are nearly synonymous with the informal urban economy, represent a substantial proportion of all economic actives. Information on traded products and types of business can be obtained from the survey. Indirectly, the data on business owners within the household, any household members involved, and the location of the enterprise operates can also shed light on the types of the businesses in which household enterprises are involved. Finally, business profits can be calculated using revenue and cost information collected through the survey questionnaire.

Indicators on the Extractive Sector

Given the increasingly significant contribution of extractive industries to national income in Sierra Leone, it is important to gain insights on the role this sector plays in the labor market. For the direct links between the extractive sector and the labor market, the International Standard Industrial Classification codes on mining and quarrying can help identify individuals employed in this sector. For

Findings from the 2014 Labor Force Survey in Sierra Leone
http://dx.doi.org/10.1596/978-1-4648-0742-8

nonfarm household enterprises, information is captured on the sectors of activity of main customers, which includes the mining and quarrying industries.

Indicators on Migration and Civil Conflict

The SLLFS captures whether respondents are native born in the districts in which they currently live, where they were born if they are not native to the districts in which they live, and how long they have lived in their current locations. The SLLFS also queries the reasons for the most recent move and the reasons for staying in a location. Employment, marriage, and community disputes are among the options. The ratio of those respondents who select work as a reason to move, divided by all who have moved either from their birth locations or from the districts of last residence, can help link migration to employment.

There is also a survey question about the ways in which respondents were affected by the civil war over the period 1991–2002. Coupled with the migration indicators, the percentage of the population that moved or stayed on one place because of the civil conflict can be calculated as a means to gauge the effect of civil conflict on location of residence. The potential effect of the conflict on labor market outcomes is also assessed by comparing basic labor market indicators— that is, the labor force participation rate, the unemployment rate, the time-related underemployment rate, and the inactivity rate—on respondents who declared they were affected by the conflict and respondents who declared they were not affected by the conflict.

Indicators of Youth Employment

Besides calculating key labor market indicators separately on the youth population, additional indicators can be analyzed to help clarify the employment status of youth. One set of such indicators focuses on skills by comparing the educational background, literacy, school attendance, and educational attainment of the youth population and older cohorts. Whether or not individual youth have served apprenticeships, the areas of work during apprenticeship, the most recent areas of vocational training undergone, and the duration of training are also analyzed. In the absence of panel data, a cross-sectional snapshot of the proportion of youth in school only, working only, both working and in school, and neither working nor in school is used to examine the transition from school to work by age cohort. Key labor market indicators and income data can be compared on youth who have not undergone training and youth who have undertaken technical and vocational education and training or who have served apprenticeships. A similar comparison can be made across youth pursuing training in different fields.

Besides constraints in skills and education, youth also face financial constraints, especially self-employed youth in the nonfarm sector. Indicators of access to finance and credit such as information on the sources and amounts of start-up capital required, access to credit, business credit, and emergency credit in the previous 12 months are included in the analysis. A few other issues are critical to youth employment. One is the gender differences in outcomes and constraints, which can be analyzed using information on key labor market outcomes, occupational choice variables, time use indicators, and the reasons for absence from job, for not looking for work, for time-related underemployment. Another critical issue is family formation, which can be analyzed using information on the age, marital status, and the age at first child's birth and the associations with labor market outcomes among respondents. The coverage of employment-related social protection programs can be estimated, along with the main types of programs providing support and the supporting organizations.

Table A.1 How to Calculate Key Indicators in the 2014 SLLFS key traditional labor market indicators

Concepts	Concept subcomponents	Corresponding variables in SLLFS database
Employed	(i) Worked in the past week	Option 1 in C.2 (Confirm if respondent had any economic activity during the last completed week).
	(ii) Temporarily out of work	Options 1, 2, or 3 in D.2 (Main reasons for being absent from job), or option 1 and 2 in D.3 (Time length being away from work), or option 1 in D.4 (Receiving pay or returns while not working)
Unemployment	(i) Without employment	"No" option in D.1 (Have economic activities to return to)
	(ii) Currently available	"Yes" option in D.9 (Available to work last week or in the next two weeks)
	(iii) Seeking employment	"Yes" option in D.5 (Looked for a job or tried to start business in the last 4 weeks)
Inactive	(i) Not employed	Option 2 in C.2 (Had any economic activity in the last week)
	(ii) Not unemployed	"No" option in D.5 (Looked for a job or tried to start business in the last 4 weeks) or "No" option in D.9 (Available to work last week or in the next two weeks)
Discouraged	(i) Without employment	"No" option in D.1 (Have economic activities to return to)
	(ii) Currently available	"Yes" option in D.9 (Available to work last week or in the next two weeks)
	(iii) Not seeking employment due to labor market– related reasons	Option 5, 6, 11, and 14 in D.6 (Main reasons for not looking for work in the last 4 weeks)

table continues next page

Findings from the 2014 Labor Force Survey in Sierra Leone
http://dx.doi.org/10.1596/978-1-4648-0742-8

Table A.1 How to Calculate Key Indicators in the 2014 SLLFS key traditional labor market indicators *(continued)*

Concepts	Concept subcomponents	Corresponding variables in SLLFS database
Time-related underemployment	(i) Worked less than 8 hours per day in the last week	E.6 (Average hours per day spent on main activity) plus F.7 (Average hours per day spent on secondary activity)
	(ii) Expressed willingness to work more	Option 1 in I.1 (Wish to work more)
	(iii) Main reasons for not working more is "economic"	Options 1, 2, 3, 6, 7 in I.3 (Reasons for not working more)
Formality of employment	(i) Formality of paid employment	If an individual is in paid employment (Option 1, 2, or 8 in E.9, employment status) the job is formal if with "1" in E.12 (Type of contract) and "Yes" option in E.16 (Employer contribute to pension) and "Yes" option in E.17 (Medical benefits) are selected.
	(ii) Formality of self-employment	If an individual is in self-employment without regular employees (Option 3 or 4 in E.9, employment status) then she or he has informal employment.
Formality of nonfarm household enterprises	The enterprise is not registered	Informal if Option 6 in K.18 is selected.

other key SLLFS indicators

Group of indicators	Indicators	Corresponding variables in the 2014 SLLFS
Main sectors and types of employment	Employment distribution for primary current activities	E.9 (Employment status) combined with E.3 (International Standard Industrial Classification codes for main duties in current main job/activity)
Household agricultural activities	Type of crops grown and percent of households that grow those crops	L.18A (Crop ID)
	Type of livestock raised and percent of household raised them	L.27 (Type of animals raised)
	Landownership	L.5 (Ownership status of this plot) plus L.7 (Type of proof for ownership)
	Agricultural labor input	L.10 (HH member labor inputs), L.11 (non-HH member labor inputs), L.12 (Wage cost)
Indicators on nonfarm household enterprises	Products and services	K.2 (Main product traded or services provided, indexed by International Standard Industrial Classification codes)
	Business type	K.13 (Type of business)
	Business owner	K.3 (Owner of the business in the household)
	Household members involved	K.4 (Household members involved)
	Business location	K.5 (Location where the enterprise operates)

table continues next page

other key SLLFS indicator *(continued)*

Group of indicators	*Indicators*	*Corresponding variables in the 2014 SLLFS*
Indicators for the extractive sector	Individuals employed in this extractive sector	E.4 (Main work functions, indexed by International Standard Industrial Classification codes)
	Nonfarm household enterprises that depend on the extractive sector	K.9 (Sectors in which the nonfarm household enterprises' target customers work)
Indicators related to migration and civil conflict	Whether the individual has moved	B.19 ("Where were you born?"), B.20 ("How long have you been living here?"), B.21 ("Where were you living before coming here?") for SLLFS-eligible individuals
	Main reasons for migration	B.22 ("What was your main reason for moving here?"), B.23 ("What is your main reason for staying here, and not moving back to where you came from?")
	Whether the individual is affected by the civil war	B.18 ("In what way were you affected by the Civil (Rebel) War in the period from 1991 to 2002?")
Indicators related to youth employment	Basic education background	B.1 (Literacy), B.2 (School attendance), B.5 (Educational attainment)
	Apprenticeship and technical and vocational education and training experiences	B.16 (Whether or not the individual has done an apprenticeship), B.17 (Areas of work during apprenticeship), B.10 (Subjects taken during the last vocational training), B.11 (Training duration)
	School-to-work transition snapshot by age	A.6 (Age), B.7 (Currently in school), C.2 (Currently working),
	Profitability	K.8 (Total revenues), K.12 (Expenditure on wages and salary), K.14 (Cost of traded goods, K.15 (Enterprises total expenditure on raw materials/inputs per month), K.16 (Other operational costs)
	Access to finance indicators	K.19 (Start-up capital), K.20 (Start-up capital sources), K.21 (Business credit), K.22 (Emergency credit), K.23 (Emergency credit sources)
	Occupational choices between genders	E.1 (Main job and activity), E.2 (Main duties in this job and activity)
	Occupational constraints between genders	D.2 (Constraints, measured by reasons for absence from job), D.6 (Reasons for not looking for work), and I.3 (Reasons for time-related under employment), time use indicators in section J.
	Timing of family formation	A.11 (Age), A.7 (Marital status), A.11 (Age at first child's birth)
	Social protection and labor programs	A.14 (Government program participation), A.15 (Supporting organization)

table continues next page

Findings from the 2014 Labor Force Survey in Sierra Leone
http://dx.doi.org/10.1596/978-1-4648-0742-8

other key SLLFS indicator *(continued)*

Skills	Years of schooling	B.5 (Highest level of education completed). Transformed to years of schooling assuming: sub-standard A=0.5 years; Standard 1 to Form 4 and SSS 2= 1 to 11 years respectively; Form 5 (GCE), Form 6 Lower/SSS 3, Form 6 Lower, Form 6 and Form 6 upper/S, Form 6 Upper and GCE(A)= 12 years; College Students, University Undergraduate Students, Certificates, Diploma and Postgraduate Diploma Students= 14 years; Bachelors Degree = 16 years; Masters Degree or Higher = 20 years.

Source: 2014 Sierra Leone Labor Force Survey.
a. The ILO definition requires the exclusion of subsistence farmers. However, the ratio of the value of goods sold to the value of goods produced is unreliable in the SLLFS, and, thus, this criterion has not been applied.

Note

1. The latest official ILO document is "Resolution Concerning Statistics of Work, Employment and Labour Underutilization," 2013, http://www.ilo.org/wcmsp5/groups/public/---dgreports/---stat/documents/normativeinstrument/wcms_230304.pdf. Unless otherwise specified, this document is the default reference for definitions of labor statistics. The SLLFS primarily follows these guidelines, but, because it is not fully designed to use this new framework, there may be limitations.

Methodology of the Statistical Analysis and Additional Results Tables

Labor Market Status

The analysis of the determinants of labor market status was undertaken using a multinomial logit model. This model considers labor market status as a result of the decision making of individuals and the hiring decisions of employers. The combination of these factors is used to calculate an index of the likelihood that a particular labor market status will be observed (its latent value), as well as the status actually observed that is associated with the highest index (the most likely). The calculation of the index is based on a set of observable characteristics, including gender, educational attainment (6 levels), household size, disability status, marital status (7 categories), age (10 age groups), and geographical location (urban Freetown, other urban areas, and rural areas), and characteristics that are not observable in the survey, but that affect the likelihood that a particular status will occur. A possible labor market status includes employed, unemployed (ILO definition), in school full time, and not in employment, unemployment, education, or training (NEET).

Table B.1 presents the marginal effects calculated from this estimation. The marginal effects presented here are calculated for a (hypothetical) person with the average characteristics of the population. The effects describe the change in the probability that a particular outcome will occur (here, a labor market status) if the variable in question changes either by 1 unit (household size) or if the indicator variable associated with the characteristic changes from 0 to 1. Thus, for example, table B.1 shows that the likelihood of being employed is 9.48 percentage points higher for a man than a woman who possesses the average values in the sample for all other variables.

Technically, the estimation is undertaken using maximum likelihood. The latent value V_i^j of outcome $j \in \{employed, unemployed, in school, NEET\}$ can be written as follows:

$$V_i^j = X_i \beta^j + \varepsilon_i^j \tag{B.1}$$

Table B.1 Marginal Effects for Multinomial Logit Model of Labor Market Status

	Employed		Unemployed		In school or training		NEET	
	Marginal effect	Std. error	Marginal effect	Std. error	Marginal effect	Std. error	Marginal effect	Std. error
Male	9.48***	0.002	0.59***	0.000	−0.0066	0.006	−10.06***	0.004
never went to school	−8.16***	0.101	−2.97***	0.007	−0.1597	0.136	11.29***	0.028
Incomplete primary	−10.16***	0.003	−1.25***	0.000	0.0058	0.005	11.40***	0.005
Completed primary	−7.65***	0.005	−1.76***	0.000	0.0097	0.008	9.40***	0.005
Completed lower secondary	−10.92***	0.008	−1.98***	0.000	0.0179	0.015	12.89***	0.009
Completed upper secondary	−17.03***	0.009	−1.57***	0.000	0.0253	0.022	18.58***	0.013
Consumption units (Adult=1, Child=0.5)	−2.81***	0.001	0.36***	0.000	0.0018	0.002	2.45***	0.001
Disabled	−10.74***	0.005	−2.02***	0.001	−0.0056	0.005	12.77***	0.002
Married (polygamous)	6.35***	0.006	−1.52***	0.000	0.0076	0.007	−4.84***	0.001
Informal/loose union	15.23***	0.012	−1.78***	0.001	−0.0200	0.017	−13.43***	0.005
Divorced	−5.69***	0.016	1.15***	0.002	−0.0266	0.022	4.56***	0.007
Separated	−4.07*	0.021	0.59***	0.001	−0.0379	0.030	3.52***	0.008
Widowed	−7.18***	0.007	−0.92***	0.001	−0.0102	0.009	8.11***	0.002
Never married	−24.52***	0.039	2.08***	0.004	0.0912	0.078	22.34***	0.036
20–24	11.07***	0.01	2.05***	0.001	−0.0186	0.016	−13.10***	0.006
25–29	18.25***	0.015	1.56***	0.001	−0.0272	0.023	−19.78***	0.008
30–34	23.69***	0.017	−0.48***	0.001	−0.0313	0.027	−23.17***	0.008
35–39	23.96***	0.016	−0.08	0.001	−0.0292	0.025	−23.85***	0.008
40–44	21.31***	0.019	0.29***	0.001	−0.0337	0.029	−21.57***	0.008
45–49	21.80***	0.019	−0.82***	0.001	−0.0327	0.028	−20.95***	0.008
50–54	18.98***	0.036	0.26	0.002	−0.0757	0.052	−19.17***	0.015
55–59	19.87***	0.028	−2.02***	0.001	−0.0547	0.040	−17.80***	0.011
60–64	12.05***	0.027	−0.84***	0.001	−0.0531	0.039	−11.16***	0.011
Freetown	−12.49***	0.003	3.11***	0.001	0.0001	0.000	9.38***	0.002
Urban other thanFreetown	−10.91***	0.002	1.52***	0.001	0.0078	0.007	9.38***	0.004
Log Likelihood = −2150962.2			Pseudo R^2 = 0.2737			Number of Observations = 3008022		

Source: 2014 Sierra Leone Labor Force Survey.

Note: Standard errors are shown in parentheses. The multinomial logit model is estimated using sample weights. The marginal effects are estimated at weighted average values for all covariates in the sample. The reference categories are female, completed postsecondary, not disabled, married (monogamous), age 15–19, rural resident.

Significance level: * = 10 percent, ** = 5 percent, *** = 1 percent.

where X_i is a set of observable characteristics, β^j is a vector of coefficients that determine how the characteristics affect the value of outcome j, and ε^j captures unobserved characteristics as a random variable distributed according to a standard type-1 extreme value distribution. The probability of observing an individual in labor market status j can be written as follows:

$$P \text{ (Labor Market State}_i = j) = P\ (V_i^j \geq V_i^{j'}),\ j' \neq j$$
$$= \exp\ (\ X_i\beta^j)/\Sigma_{k \in \{\text{Employed,Unemployed,In School,NEET}\}}$$
$$\exp\ (X_i\beta^k)' \tag{B.2}$$

where one of the coefficient vectors (β^{Employed}, here) is normalized to zero. The choice of the normalization does not affect the estimation results or the marginal effects.

The specification of the multinomial logit model implies that changing the value of the index for a particular alternative will not affect the rankings of other alternatives, a hypothesis known as independence of irrelevant alternatives. For example, if NEET becomes more attractive when a baby is born, the multinomial logit model assumes that the likelihood of employment of the individuals were they to choose not to stay home would not change. Hausman and McFadden proposed a test for this hypothesis in 1984, and the main alternative model to the multinomial logit is the multinomial probit. This model is more complicated and requires simulation techniques for estimation whenever there are more than three alternatives to choose from and, as such, can be less precise and is necessarily sensitive to other technical parameters (seed, types of draws, the simulator used) the influence of which is untestable. Although both models have been estimated, this report presents the multinomial logit results because the marginal effects resulting from each estimation technique are typically similar both qualitatively and quantitatively.

Job Type

The analysis of the determinants of the types of job was also undertaken using a multinomial logit model. For this model, the following variables were specified as determinants of the types of job: gender, educational attainment (6 levels), household size, disability status, sector of activity (agriculture, mining and extractive industries, manufacturing and utilities, construction, and services), age (10 age groups), and geographical location (urban Freetown, other urban areas, and rural areas). The job types considered were wage employment, nonagricultural household employment, agricultural household employment, and unpaid work contributions to family. Table B.2 presents the marginal effects calculated from this estimation.

Table B.2 Marginal Effects for Multinomial Logit Model of Job Types

	Wage employee		Non-agricultural household enterprise		Agricultural household enterprise		Unpaid contributing family worker	
	Marginal effect	Std. error	Marginal effect	Std. error	Marginal effect	Std. error	Marginal effect	Std. error
Male	28.52***	0.002	0.21**	0.001	0.0000***	0.000	−28.73***	0.003
Never went to school	−54.45***	0.008	11.39***	0.004	0.0000***	0.000	43.06***	0.010
Incomplete primary	−22.13***	0.002	7.19***	0.006	0.0000***	0.000	14.94***	0.007
Completed primary	−21.40***	0.002	10.02***	0.006	0.0000***	0.000	11.38***	0.008
Completed lower secondary	−18.29***	0.002	11.69***	0.007	0.0000***	0.000	6.61***	0.009
Completed upper secondary	−13.77***	0.003	7.73***	0.006	0.0000***	0.000	6.04***	0.009
Disabled	−1.58***	0.005	−2.95***	0.002	0.0000***	0.000	4.53***	0.006
Agriculture	−1.26***	0.001	−90.05***	0.000	0.0001***	0.000	91.31***	0.001
Mining and extractive industries	4.87***	0.006	−6.14***	0.002	−0.0001***	0.000	1.27***	0.007
Manufacturing and utilities	−13.96***	0.002	−5.03***	0.002	−6.1406***	0.001	25.13***	0.002
Construction	20.56***	0.015	−3.07***	0.002	0.0000***	0.000	−17.49***	0.016
20–24	33.96***	0.006	2.20***	0.002	0.0000***	0.000	−36.16***	0.006
25–29	27.35***	0.006	6.74***	0.003	0.0000***	0.000	−34.09***	0.006
30–34	56.21***	0.006	8.24***	0.003	0.0000***	0.000	−64.45***	0.004
35–39	36.15***	0.006	8.30***	0.003	0.0000***	0.000	−44.45***	0.006
40–44	42.92***	0.006	2.76***	0.002	0.0000***	0.000	−45.67***	0.006
45–49	43.57***	0.007	11.36***	0.004	0.0000***	0.000	−54.93***	0.005
50–54	29.87***	0.007	4.25***	0.002	0.0000***	0.000	−34.12***	0.007
55–59	35.33***	0.008	2.76***	0.002	0.0000***	0.000	−38.09***	0.008
60–64	19.09***	0.009	3.46***	0.003	0.0000***	0.000	−22.55***	0.009
Freetown	22.60***	0.005	−2.72***	0.001	0.0000***	0.000	−19.88***	0.005
Urban other than Freetown	13.11***	0.003	−0.84***	0.001	0.0000***	0.000	−12.27***	0.004
Log Likelihood = −713428			Pseudo R^2 = 0.6432				Number of Observations = 1854347	

Source: 2014 Sierra Leone Labor Force Survey.

Note: Standard errors are shown in parentheses. The multinomial logit is estimated on the sample of employed individuals using sample weights. The reference categories are female, completed postsecondary, not disabled, service sector, age 15–19, rural resident.

Significance level: * = 10 percent, ** = 5 percent, *** = 1 percent

Labor Earnings

The analysis of the determinants of labor market earnings was undertaken using a log-linear regression with a correction for potential selection bias. In this model, the log of current earnings from the main job (for wage employees, including paid apprentices) is regressed on a series of determinants of wage income comprisng the following variables: gender, educational attainment (6 levels), disability status, type of employer (private sector, public sector, or NGO or international organization), sector of activity (agriculture, mining and extractive industries, manufacturing and utilities, construction, and services), age (10 age groups), and geographical location (urban Freetown, other urban areas, and rural areas). However, as the analysis of labor market status and job type highlight, the people who are employed as wage workers (and thus participate in the regression) do not represent a random sample of the population, even if the labor force survey does sample the population randomly (whenever weights are applied). Because the characteristics that make people more likely to obtain a wage job may also be associated with higher earnings (higher education, for example), estimates of the effects of these characteristics and all other coefficients in the model are biased. James Heckman proposed a technique for correcting for this selection bias in 1979 that relies on estimating a separate model for the likelihood that an individual is a wage employee. These estimates are then used to correct for the bias in the earnings regression. In the context of the analysis presented in table B.3, the following variables have been included in the model: gender, educational attainment (6 levels), household size, disability status, marital status (7 categories), age (10 age groups), and geographical location (urban Freetown, other urban areas, and rural areas). Certain variables (type of employer, sector of activity) are not included in the model that explains whether or not an individual is a wage employee because these variables do not exist among people who are not working. Conversely, variables such as marital status or household size are assumed not to affect earnings directly, although they do have an indirect effect in that they influence which people are actually wage employees.

Technically, the estimation is undertaken by simultaneously estimating a log linear earnings equation and a probit model. A probit model estimates the

Table B.3 Heckman Selection-Corrected Regressions of Log Earnings in Main Job

Log Earnings	Wage Employees	Nonagricultural Self-Employment	Agricultural Self-Employment
Male	1.069*** (0.012)	0.962*** (0.020)	0.668*** (0.024)
Never went to school	−4.573*** (0.023)	0.428*** (0.031)	−0.945*** (0.119)
Incomplete primary	−3.919*** (0.030)	0.164*** (0.037)	−0.631*** (0.125)
Completed primary	−3.257*** (0.022)	−0.118*** (0.036)	−1.009*** (0.125)

table continues next page

Findings from the 2014 Labor Force Survey in Sierra Leone
http://dx.doi.org/10.1596/978-1-4648-0742-8

Table B.3 Heckman Selection-Corrected Regressions of Log Earnings in Main Job *(continued)*

Log Earnings	Wage Employees	Nonagricultural Self-Employment	Agricultural Self-Employment
Completed lower secondary	−2.749*** (0.019)	−0.037 (0.034)	−0.727*** (0.128)
Completed upper secondary	−1.923*** −0.017	0.043 (0.035)	−1.340*** (0.126)
Disabled	−0.135*** (0.032)	0.992*** (0.055)	−0.591*** (0.075)
Public Sector	−0.199*** (0.010)		
NGO or International Organization	−0.075*** (0.014)		
Agriculture	−0.214*** (0.019)		0.314*** (0.079)
Mining and Extractives	0.350*** (0.015)	0.528*** (0.063)	
Manufacturing and Utilities	−0.274*** (0.017)	0.233*** (0.031)	
Construction	0.432*** (0.016)	−0.828*** (0.054)	
20–24	1.109*** (0.033)	−0.385*** (0.041)	0.299*** (0.059)
25–29	1.990*** (0.034)	−0.657*** (0.044)	0.833*** (0.055)
30–34	2.377*** (0.035)	−0.343*** (0.044)	0.839*** (0.050)
35–39	1.898*** (0.035)	−0.818*** (0.045)	−0.137*** (0.052)
40–44	2.823*** (0.035)	−0.939*** (0.045)	0.436*** (0.066)
45–49	2.323*** (0.036)	−0.817*** (0.046)	0.658*** (0.055)
50–54	2.319*** (0.038)	−0.422*** (0.048)	0.976*** (0.053)
55–59	2.921*** (0.039)	−1.815*** (0.049)	0.96*** (0.073)
60–64	1.570*** (0.045)	−0.832*** (0.059)	−1.141*** (0.067)
Freetown	2.467*** (0.016)	0.003 (0.026)	
Urban other than Freetown	1.336*** (0.014)	−0.375*** (0.021)	−0.347*** (0.039)
Constant	8.039*** (0.042)	15.850*** (0.090)	11.360*** (0.191)

table continues next page

Findings from the 2014 Labor Force Survey in Sierra Leone
http://dx.doi.org/10.1596/978-1-4648-0742-8

Table B.3 Heckman Selection-Corrected Regressions of Log Earnings in Main Job *(continued)*

Selection into Employment	Wage employees	Non-agricultural self-Employment	Agricultural self-employment
Male	0.567 ***	−0.497 ***	−0.026 ***
	(0.003)	(0.005)	(0.006)
Never Went to School	−1.773 ***	0.232 ***	0.440 ***
	(0.006)	(0.010)	−0.029
Incomplete Primary	−1.573 ***	0.410 ***	0.484 ***
	(0.008)	(0.012)	−0.03
Completed Primary	−1.284 ***	0.276 ***	0.206 ***
	(0.007)	(0.011)	−0.03
Completed Lower Secondary	−1.043 ***	0.465 ***	0.183 ***
	(0.006)	(0.011)	−0.03
Completed Upper Secondary	−0.773 ***	0.275 ***	0.447 ***
	(0.006)	(0.011)	−0.03
Number of Consumption Units (Adults=1, Children=0.5 Units)	−0.054 ***	0.067 ***	0.136 ***
	(0.001)	(0.001)	−0.001
Disabled	−0.017 *	−0.342 ***	−0.272 ***
	(0.009)	(0.017)	−0.019
Married(polygamous)	0.000	−0.278 ***	−0.353 ***
	(0.005)	(0.011)	−0.014
Informal/Loose Union	0.146 ***	0.130 ***	−4.941 ***
	(0.011)	(0.016)	−600.5
Divorced	0.239 ***	0.021 ***	−5.608 ***
	(0.013)	(0.017)	−1107
Separated	0.075 ***	0.619 ***	−0.436 ***
	(0.007)	(0.008)	−0.019
Widowed	0.104 ***	−0.280 ***	−0.217 ***
	(0.007)	(0.010)	−0.012
Never Married	−0.022 ***	−0.390 ***	−0.378 ***
	(0.003)	(0.006)	−0.009
20-24	0.802 ***	0.576 ***	0.229 ***
	(0.008)	(0.011)	−0.012
25-29	1.072 ***	0.917 ***	0.596 ***
	(0.008)	(0.011)	−0.011
30-34	1.484 ***	1.121 ***	0.373 ***
	(0.008)	(0.011)	−0.013
35-39	1.241 ***	0.954 ***	0.61 ***
	(0.009)	(0.011)	−0.012
40-44	1.535 ***	1.023 ***	0.037 ***
	(0.009)	(0.012)	−0.016
45-49	1.292 ***	1.151 ***	0.466 ***
	(0.009)	(0.012)	−0.014
50-54	1.275 ***	1.286 ***	0.801 ***
	(0.010)	(0.013)	−0.014
55-59	1.449 ***	1.055 ***	0.27 ***
	(0.010)	(0.014)	−0.018

table continues next page

Findings from the 2014 Labor Force Survey in Sierra Leone
http://dx.doi.org/10.1596/978-1-4648-0742-8

Table B.3 Heckman Selection-Corrected Regressions of Log Earnings in Main Job (continued)

Selection into Employment	Wage employees	Non-agricultural self-Employment	Agricultural self-employment
60-64	1.021 ***	0.572 ***	0.247 ***
	(0.012	−0.018	−0.018
Freetown	0.720 ***	1.211 ***	−6.032
	(0.004	−0.006	−1177
Urban Other Than Freetown	0.503 ***	0.906 ***	−0.573 ***
	(0.004	−0.005	−0.008
Constant	−1.848 ***	−3.512 ***	−3.118 ***
	(0.010)	−0.015	−0.031
ath(r)	1.659 ***	−0.776 ***	0.515 ***
	(0.006)	−0.014	−0.028
Ln(s)	1.012 ***	0.58 ***	0.484 ***
	(0.003)	−0.007	−0.011
Observations	2,976,562	1,997,376	
Number of Observations	2,977,000	1,997,000	
Number of Uncensored Observations	155,432	31,707	
Pseudo Log-likelihood	−700,168	−193,259	

Source: 2014 Sierra Leone Labor Force Survey.
Note: Standard errors are shown in parentheses. The Heckman selection model is estimated by maximum likelihood using sample weights. The reference categories are female, completed postsecondary, not disabled, service sector, age 15–19, rural resident.
Significance level: * = 10 percent, ** = 5 percent, *** = 1 percent

probability of an event occurring as a function of observable characteristics; in this case, the event is status as a wage employee. A latent index describes the factors that make a person more likely to obtain a wage job, and, if this index crosses a threshold (typically zero), the outcome is observed, as follows:

$$s_i = Z_i \gamma + \varepsilon_i \tag{B.3}$$
$$P \text{ (Wage Employee}_i) = P (s_i \geq 0) = P (Z_i\gamma \geq - \varepsilon_i) = \Phi (Z_i\gamma), \tag{B.4}$$

where ε_i is assumed to have a standard normal distribution, and Φ is the cumulative distribution function for a standard normal random variable. Heckman (1979) showed that introducing the expected value of ε_i into the wage equation captures all the bias that would otherwise affect the model coefficients, and the expected value of ε_i can be written as a function of Z_i, the inverse Mills ratio, namely:

$$\lambda(Z_i\hat{\gamma}) = \frac{\phi (Z_i\hat{\gamma})}{\Phi (Z_i\hat{\gamma})} \tag{B.5}$$

where $\hat{\gamma}$ is the probit estimate of γ, and ϕ is the density function of a standard normal random variable. This estimation can also be performed in two steps (first, the probit and, second, the log linear regression with extra variable), but simultaneous estimation is more efficient.

Migration

The analysis of the determinants of migration was undertaken using a multinomial logit model. For this model, the following variables were specified as determinants of the reason for migration: gender, educational attainment (6 levels), displaced during the civil conflict, otherwise affected by the civil conflict, landownership, disability status, age (10 age groups), and geographical location (urban Freetown, other urban areas, and rural areas). The reasons for migration considered were nonmigrant, migrant for marriage, migrant for work, migrant for education, and migrant for other reasons. table B.4 presents the marginal effects calculated from this estimation. The variable considered is whether the individual is a migrant, that is, living in a district different from the district of birth. Given that the survey took place in 2013, people had time to return to their home districts even if they had been displaced by the conflict; it is thus reasonable to consider displacement during the war as a potential motive for currently residing outside the home district, and this variable may not represent a motive for migration years after the end of the conflict.

Formality

The analysis of the determinants of formal employment was undertaken using a selection bias–corrected probit model (table B.5). The probit estimation and selection bias correction are both similar to the procedure described for the earnings estimation, although a probit model (formal vs. informal) wage is used as the main equation instead of log earnings. The determinants of this probit model are gender, educational attainment (6 levels), disability status, sector of activity (agriculture, mining and extractive industries, manufacturing and utilities, construction, and services), age (10 age groups), and geographical location (urban Freetown, other urban areas, and rural areas). The selection equation, which, in this case, concerns whether or not the individual was employed, was based on the following variables: gender, educational attainment (6 levels), household size, disability status, marital status (7 categories), age (10 age groups), and geographical location (urban Freetown, other urban areas, and rural areas). The selection bias–corrected probit model is estimated by the maximum likelihood.

Educational Attainment

The analysis of the determinants of the level of education was undertaken using an ordered probit (table B.6). This type of model is used if the outcome being studied (in this case, the level of education) is naturally ordered (for instance, incomplete primary is less education than completed upper secondary), but the variable is measured in categories instead of numbers with a strict cardinal interpretation. In the case of educational categories, the following situation

Table B.4 Marginal Effects for Multinomial Logit Model of Reasons for Migration

	Marriage		Work		School		Other	
	Marginal Effect	Std. Error	Marginal Effect	Std. Error	Marginal Effect	Std. Error	Marginal Effect	Std. Error
Male	-3.15***	0.006	0.62***	0.351	0.0006	0.002***	0.64	0.005
Never went to school	-4.39***	0.034	-0.64***	0.364	-0.0049	0.017***	0.38	0.002
Incomplete primary	-2.40***	0.006	-0.14***	0.082	-0.0005	0.002***	3.33	0.005
Completed primary	-1.94***	0.006	-0.13***	0.073	-0.0005	0.002***	0.99	0.002
Completed lower secondary	-2.71***	0.008	-0.28***	0.160	-0.0006	0.002***	3.16	0.003
Completed upper secondary	-2.64***	0.007	-0.18***	0.102	-0.0002	0.001***	1.76	0.002
Displaced by the civil war	-0.50***	0.007	-0.31***	0.179	0.0006	0.002***	-0.41	0.002
Affected by the civil war (other than displacement)	-0.77***	0.013	-0.46***	0.264	0.0004	0.001***	-0.87	0.006
Land owner	-2.21***	0.053	-1.54***	0.868	-0.0011	0.004***	-1.42	0.021
Disabled	0.01***	0.017	0.78***	0.444	-0.0009	0.003***	-0.46	0.002
Married (polygamous)	-2.42***	0.007	-0.18***	0.104	-0.0005	0.002***	0.00	0.001
Informal/loose union	6.46***	0.007	-0.37***	0.145	-0.0005	0.002***	-1.00	0.001
Divorced	-1.70***	0.006	-0.37***	0.154	-0.0005	0.002***	-0.72	0.002
Separated	-2.70***	0.005	0.06***	0.037	-0.0007	0.002***	-0.52	0.001
Widowed	0.44***	0.003	-0.16***	0.093	-0.0012	0.002***	-0.71	0.002
Never married	-3.12***	0.014	-0.55***	0.317	-0.0001	0***	1.25	0.003
20–24	0.72***	0.008	-0.37***	0.210	-0.0006	0.002***	7.19	0.005
25–29	1.01***	0.006	-0.31***	0.176	-0.0005	0.002***	7.06	0.004
30–34	0.25***	0.007	-0.32***	0.182	-0.0006	0.002***	21.71	0.010
35–39	4.41***	0.005	-0.35***	0.200	-0.0005	0.002***	13.34	0.007
40–44	1.55***	0.008	-0.41***	0.234	-0.0044	0.014***	19.38	0.010

table continues next page

Table B.4 Marginal Effects for Multinomial Logit Model of Reasons for Migration (continued)

	Marriage		Work		School		Other	
	Marginal Effect	Std. Error	Marginal Effect	Std. Error	Marginal Effect	Std. Error	Marginal Effect	Std. Error
45–49	1.77***	0.005	−0.27***	0.156	−0.0004***	0.001	27.34***	0.012
50–54	−1.18***	0.005	−0.19***	0.110	−0.0004***	0.001	35.94***	0.035
55–59	−2.50***	0.008	−0.30***	0.171	−0.0006***	0.002	42.56***	0.017
60–64	2.42***	0.003	−0.19***	0.110	−0.0002***	0.001	21.30***	0.022
Freetown	6.65***	0.043	0.26***	0.147	0.0877***	0.302	14.84***	0.070
Urban other than Freetown	2.19***	0.018	0.42***	0.238	0.0094***	0.032	0.75***	0.005
Log Likelihood = −439531			Pseudo R^2 = 0.1235				Number of Observations = 1349131	

Source: 2014 Sierra Leone Labor Force Survey.

Note: Standard errors are shown in parentheses. The multinomial logit model is estimated using sample weights. The marginal effects are estimated at weighted average values for all covariates in the sample. The reference categories are female, completed postsecondary, not disabled, not affected by the war, not a landowner, married (monogamous), age 15–19, rural resident.

Significance level: * = 10 percent, ** = 5 percent, *** = 1 percent

Table B.5   **Selection-Corrected Probit Models of Formality**

	Wage employment		Non-agricultural self employment	
	Formality	Selection	Formality	Selection
Male	0.270***	0.639***	0.551***	−0.273***
	(0.011)	(0.003)	(0.008)	(0.002)
Never went to school	−2.341***	−1.815***	−0.415***	0.905***
	(0.012)	(0.006)	(0.023)	(0.008)
Incomplete primary	−1.904***	−1.556***	−0.224***	1.125***
	(0.015)	(0.008)	(0.026)	(0.008)
Completed primary	−1.416***	−1.327***	−0.173***	1.093***
	(0.013)	(0.007)	(0.025)	(0.008)
Completed lower secondary	−1.351***	−1.095***	0.008	1.103***
	(0.010)	(0.006)	(0.024)	(0.008)
Completed upper secondary	−0.853***	−0.815***	−0.081***	0.792***
	(0.011)	(0.006)	(0.023)	(0.008)
Number of consumption units		−0.058***		−0.020***
		(0.001)		(0.001)
Disabled	−0.176***	−0.019***	−0.127***	−0.008
	(0.020)	(0.009)	(0.017)	(0.006)
Married (polygamous)		0.005		0.081***
		(0.006)		(0.004)
Informal / loose union		0.251***		0.427***
		(0.013)		(0.009)
Divorced		0.213***		−0.133
		(0.016)		(0.011)
Separated		0.204***		0.348***
		(0.008)		(0.005)
Widowed		0.020***		0.035***
		(0.009)		(0.005)
Never married		−0.180***		−0.474***
		(0.004)		(0.003)
Age 20–24	1.097***	0.750***	0.260***	0.355***
	(0.024)	(0.008)	(0.017)	(0.004)
Age 25–29	1.699***	0.975***	0.218***	0.678***
	(0.024)	(0.008)	(0.020)	(0.004)
Age 30–34	2.128	1.410***	0.642***	0.792***
	(0.024)	(0.008)	(0.021)	(0.004)
Age 35–39	1.726***	1.123***	0.631***	0.743***
	(0.024)	(0.009)	(0.020)	(0.005)
Age 40–44	2.348***	1.378***	0.633***	0.735***
	(0.025)	(0.009)	(0.021)	(0.005)
Age 45–49	2.033***	1.137***	0.743***	0.726***
	(0.025)	(0.009)	(0.021)	(0.005)
Age 50–54	2.313***	1.171***	0.666***	0.757***
	(0.027	(0.010)	(0.022)	(0.005)

table continues next page

Table B.5 Selection-Corrected Probit Models of Formality (continued)

	Wage employment		Non-agricultural self employment	
	Formality	Selection	Formality	Selection
Age 55–59	2.694***	1.292***	0.474***	0.627***
	(0.030)	(0.011)	(0.022)	(0.006)
Age 60–64	2.060***	0.886***	0.700***	0.502***
	(0.032)	(0.012)	(0.022	(0.006)
Freetown	0.451***	0.805***	0.919***	0.673***
	(0.012)	(0.004)	(0.010)	(0.003)
Other Urban Areas	0.606***	0.569***	0.922***	0.582***
	(0.008)	(0.004)	(0.008)	(0.002)
Agriculture, Fishing and Forestry	−158,602***			
	(0.000)			
Mining and Extractive Industries	−0.563***		0.257***	
	(0.014)		(0.014)	
Manufacturing and Utilities	−0.002		−0.087***	
	(0.012)		(0.011)	
Construction	−0.510***		−0.785***	
	(0.013)		(0.025)	
Constant	−1.881***	−1.705***	−2.333***	−2.396***
	(0.039)	(0.011)	(0.053)	(0.009)
Rho	0.745		0.154***	
	(0.128)			
Log Likelihood	−496057.9		−1314952	
Observations	2,985,279		2,928,247	

Source: 2014 Sierra Leone Labor Force Survey.
Note: Standard errors are shown in parentheses. The probit models are corrected for selection into wage employment or nonagricultural self-employment using sample weights. The reference categories are female, completed postsecondary, not disabled, service sector, age 15–19, rural resident.
Significance level: * = 10 percent, ** = 5 percent, *** = 1 percent

holds: although one may say that a 60-year-old is three times as old as a 20-year-old (strict cardinal interpretation), one may say that a completed lower-secondary education is three times greater than incomplete primary, even if the former is coded in the data as a 3 and the latter is coded as a 1. As with a probit model, an ordered probit model estimates an index that determines how much education an individual obtains, but, in this case, the individual receives more and more education as the index passes higher and higher thresholds. For this model, the following variables were specified as determinants of educational attainment: gender, severely affected by the conflict, disability status, marital status (7 categories), age (10 age groups), and geographical location (urban Freetown, other urban areas, and rural areas). The education levels considered are as follows: never went to school, incomplete primary, completed primary, completed lower secondary, completed upper secondary, and completed postsecondary.

Findings from the 2014 Labor Force Survey in Sierra Leone
http://dx.doi.org/10.1596/978-1-4648-0742-8

Table B.6 Marginal Effects for Ordered Probit Model of Educational Attainment

	Never went to school		Incomplete primary		Completed primary	
	Marginal effect	Std. error	Marginal effect	Std. error	Marginal effect	Std. error
Male	−14.61***	0.11	−1.18***	0.01	−0.09***	0.01
Severely affected	−0.48***	0.14	−0.04***	0.01	0.00***	0.00
Disabled	7.36***	0.36	0.41***	0.01	−0.41***	0.04
Married (polygamous)	15.37***	0.39	0.54***	0.01	−1.55***	0.07
Informal/loose union	−21.94***	0.31	−3.51***	0.09	−5.33***	0.20
Divorced	−1.31**	0.65	−0.11*	0.06	−0.01***	0.01
Separated	−5.18***	0.34	−0.48***	0.04	−0.19***	0.03
Widowed	8.87***	0.39	0.47***	0.01	−0.56***	0.05
Never married	−22.92***	0.15	−1.91***	0.02	−0.39***	0.02
20–24	−13.47***	0.14	−1.42***	0.02	−0.97***	0.03
25–29	−11.96***	0.17	−1.26***	0.02	−0.83***	0.03
30–34	−7.15***	0.23	−0.69***	0.03	−0.31***	0.02
35–39	0.99***	0.33	0.07***	0.02	−0.01***	0.01
40–44	−2.69***	0.44	−0.23***	0.04	−0.04***	0.02
45–49	0.92**	0.46	0.07**	0.03	−0.01***	0.01
50–54	3.26***	0.50	0.22***	0.03	−0.09***	0.03
55–59	5.54***	0.55	0.34***	0.03	−0.24***	0.04
60–64	16.09***	0.65	0.52***	0.01	−1.71***	0.13
Urban other than Freetown	8.18***	0.33	0.72***	0.03	0.18***	0.02

table continues next page

Table B.6 Marginal Effects for Ordered Probit Model of Educational Attainment *(continued)*

	Completed lower secondary		Completed upper secondary		Completed postsecondary	
	Marginal effect	Std. error	Marginal effect	Std. error	Marginal effect	Std. error
Male	5.10***	0.04	7.59***	0.06	3.20***	0.03
Severely affected	0.17***	0.05	0.24***	0.07	0.10***	0.03
Disabled	−2.76***	0.14	−3.40***	0.15	−1.22***	0.05
Married (polygamous)	−5.88***	0.15	−6.39***	0.13	−2.08***	0.04
Informal/loose union	3.92***	0.08	15.41***	0.28	11.44***	0.39
Divorced	0.46**	0.23	0.68**	0.34	0.28*	0.14
Separated	1.76***	0.11	2.84***	0.20	1.25***	0.10
Widowed	−3.34***	0.15	−4.02***	0.15	−1.42***	0.05
Never married	7.74***	0.06	12.07***	0.09	5.41***	0.05
20–24	4.28***	0.04	7.80***	0.10	3.78***	0.06
25–29	3.83***	0.05	6.91***	0.12	3.32***	0.07
30–34	2.40***	0.07	3.97***	0.14	1.78***	0.07
35–39	−0.36***	0.12	−0.50***	0.16	−0.20***	0.06
40–44	0.94***	0.15	1.42***	0.24	0.59***	0.11
45–49	−0.33**	0.17	−0.46**	0.23	−0.18**	0.09
50–54	−1.19***	0.19	−1.59***	0.24	−0.61	0.09
55–59	−2.05***	0.21	−2.62***	0.24	−0.96	0.08
60–64	−6.17***	0.25	−6.61***	0.21	−2.13	0.06
Urban other than Freetown	−2.83***	0.11	−4.38***	0.19	−1.88	0.09
Log Likelihood = −792891.56			Pseudo R^2 = 0.0502		Number of Observations = 516595	

Source: 2014 Sierra Leone Labor Force Survey.

ILO Definitions

Below, unless otherwise noted, are the official definitions of key labor market indicators in the resolution document of the 19th International Conference of Labor Statisticians (ICLS), "Resolution Concerning Statistics of Work, Employment and Labour Underutilization". The paragraph numbers correspond to the paragraph numbers in the original document.

Paragraph 65. To determine the working-age population:

a)   the lower age limit should be set taking into consideration the minimum age for employment and exceptions specified in national laws or regulations, or the age of completion of compulsory schooling;
b)   no upper age limit should be set, so as to permit comprehensive coverage of work activities of the adult population and to examine transitions between employment and retirement.

Paragraph 15. Persons may be classified in a short reference period, as specified in paragraph 19(a), according to their labour force status as being:

a)   in employment, as defined in paragraph 27;
b)   in unemployment, as defined in paragraph 47; or
c)   outside the labour force as defined in paragraph 16; and among these, in the potential labour force, as defined in paragraph 51.

Paragraph 27: Persons in employment are defined as all those of working age who, during a short reference period, were engaged in any activity to produce goods or provide services for pay or profit. They comprise:

a)   employed persons "at work", i.e. who worked in a job for at least one hour;
b)   employed persons "not at work" due to temporary absence from a job, or to working-time arrangements (such as shift work, flexitime and compensatory leave for overtime).

Paragraph 47. Persons in unemployment are defined as all those of working age who were not in employment, carried out activities to seek employment during a specified recent period and were currently available to take up employment given a job opportunity, where:

a) "not in employment" is assessed with respect to the short reference period for the measurement of employment;

b) to "seek employment" refers to any activity when carried out, during a specified recent period comprising the last four weeks or one month, for the purpose of finding a job or setting up a business or agricultural undertaking. This includes also part-time, informal, temporary, seasonal or casual employment, within the national territory or abroad. Examples of such activities are:
   i.   arranging for financial resources, applying for permits, licenses;
   ii. looking for land, premises, machinery, supplies, farming inputs;
   iii. seeking the assistance of friends, relatives or other types of intermediaries;
   iv. registering with or contacting public or private employment services;
   v.   applying to employers directly, checking at worksites, farms, factory gates, markets or other assembly places;
   vi. placing or answering newspaper or online job advertisements;
   vii. placing or updating résumés on professional or social networking sites online;

c) the point when the enterprise starts to exist should be used to distinguish between search activities aimed at setting up a business and the work activity itself, as evidenced by the enterprise's registration to operate or by when financial resources become available, the necessary infrastructure or materials are in place or the first client or order is received,

d) depending on the context; "currently available" serves as a test of readiness to start a job in the present, assessed with respect to a short reference period comprising that used to measure employment: (i) depending on national circumstances, the reference period may be extended to include a short subsequent period not exceeding two weeks in total, so as to ensure adequate coverage of unemployment situations among different population groups.

Paragraph 51. Potential labour force is defined as all persons of working age who, during the short reference period, were neither in employment nor in unemployment and:

a) carried out activities to "seek employment", were not "currently available" but would become available within a short subsequent period established in the light of national circumstances (i.e. unavailable jobseekers); or

b) did not carry out activities to "seek employment", but wanted employment and were "currently available" (i.e. available potential jobseekers).

Paragraph 52. Among those in paragraph 51(b) it may be useful to identify separately discouraged jobseekers, comprising those who did not "seek employment" for labour market-related reasons as listed in paragraph 80(b).

Paragraph 73(c). Measures of labour underutilization, of which more than one amongst the following headline indicators is needed so as to reflect the nature of underutilization in different settings and phases of the economic cycle:

LU1: Unemployment rate: [persons in unemployment/labour force] x 100

LU2: Combined rate of time-related underemployment and unemployment: [(persons in time-related underemployment + persons in unemployment)/ labour force] x 100

LU3: Combined rate of unemployment and potential labour force: [(persons in unemployment + potential labour force)/(extended labour force)] x 100

LU4: Composite measure of labour underutilization: [(persons in time-related underemployment + persons in unemployment + potential labour force)/(extended labour force)] x 100

Paragraph 80. For analysis of persons outside the labour force, the following alternative classifications may be used separately or in combination to shed light on specific subgroups affected by discouragement or by gender-based, economic or social barriers to employment:

(a) degree of labour market attachment of persons outside the labour force:
    (i) persons "seeking employment" but not "currently available";
    (ii) persons not "seeking employment" but "currently available";
    (iii) persons neither "seeking employment" nor "currently available" but who want employment;
    (iv) persons neither "seeking employment" nor "currently available" who do not want employment;
(b) main reason for not "seeking employment", not being "currently available" or not wanting employment: personal reasons (own illness, disability, studies); family-related reasons (pregnancy, presence of small children, refusal by family); labour market reasons (past failure to find a suitable job, lack of experience, qualifications or jobs matching the person's skills, lack of jobs in the area, considered too young or too old by prospective employers); lack of infrastructure (assets, roads, transportation, employment services); other sources of income (pensions, rents); social exclusion;
(c) main activity status, as self-declared, in the following categories: own-use production of goods; own-use provision of services; unpaid trainee work; volunteer work; studies; self-care (due to illness or disability); leisure activities (social, cultural, recreational).

Paragraph 40(a). Time-related underemployment [is] when the working time of persons in employment is insufficient in relation to alternative employment situations in which they are willing and available to engage.

Paragraph 19. The various forms of work are measured with respect to a short reference period. The appropriate reference period for each form is based on the intensity of participation and working time arrangements:

a) seven days or one week, for employment and unpaid trainee work;
b) four weeks or one calendar month, for own-use production of goods, unpaid trainee work and volunteer work;
c) one or more 24-hour days within a seven-day or one-week period, for own-use provision of services.

Paragraph 21. A person is considered to have engaged in a given form of work when performing such form of work for at least one hour during the relevant, short reference period. Use of this one-hour criterion ensures coverage of all the activities engaged in, including part-time, temporary, casual or sporadic activities, as well as comprehensive measurement of all inputs of labour into production.
    Paragraph 3 of the 17th ICLS Guidelines concerning statistical definition of informal employment

1) Informal employment comprises the total number of informal jobs as defined in subparagraphs (2) to (5) below, whether carried out in formal sector enterprises, informal sector enterprises, or households, during a given reference period.
2) As shown in the attached matrix, informal employment includes the following types of jobs: (i) own-account workers employed in their own informal sector enterprises (cell 3); (ii) employers employed in their own informal sector enterprises (cell 4); (iii) contributing family workers, irrespective of whether they work in formal or informal sector enterprises (cells 1 and 5); (iv) members of informal producers' cooperatives (cell 8); (v) employees holding informal jobs (as defined in subparagraph (5) below) in formal sector enterprises, informal sector enterprises, or as paid domestic workers employed by households (cells 2, 6 and 10); (vi) own-account workers engaged in the production of goods exclusively for own final use by their household (cell 9), if considered employed according to paragraph 9(6) of the resolution concerning statistics of the economically active population, employment, unemployment and underemployment adopted by the 13th ICLS.
3) Own-account workers, employers, members of producers' cooperatives, contributing family workers, and employees are defined in accordance with the latest version of the International Classification of Status in Employment (ICSE).
4) Producers' cooperatives are considered informal if they are not formally established as legal entities and also meet the other criteria of informal sector enterprises specified in the resolution concerning statistics of employment in the informal sector adopted by the 15th ICLS.

5) Employees are considered to have informal jobs if their employment relationship is, in law or in practice, not subject to national labour legislation, income taxation, social protection or entitlement to certain employment benefits (advance notice of dismissal, severance pay, paid annual or sick leave, etc.). The reasons may be the following: non-declaration of the jobs or the employees; casual jobs or jobs of a limited short duration; jobs with hours of work or wages below a specified threshold (e.g. for social security contributions); employment by unincorporated enterprises or by persons in households; jobs where the employee's place of work is outside the premises of the employer's enterprise (e.g. outworkers without employment contract); or jobs for which labour regulations are not applied, not enforced, or not complied with for any other reason. The operational criteria for defining informal jobs of employees are to be determined in accordance with national circumstances and data availability.

6) For purposes of analysis and policy-making, it may be useful to disaggregate the different types of informal jobs listed in paragraph 3(2) above, especially those held by employees. Such a typology and definitions should be developed as part of further work on classifications by status in employment at the international and national levels.

Findings from the 2014 Labor Force Survey in Sierra Leone
http://dx.doi.org/10.1596/978-1-4648-0742-8

ECO-AUDIT

Environmental Benefits Statement

The World Bank Group is committed to reducing its environmental footprint. In support of this commitment, the Publishing and Knowledge Division leverages electronic publishing options and print-on-demand technology, which is located in regional hubs worldwide. Together, these initiatives enable print runs to be lowered and shipping distances decreased, resulting in reduced paper consumption, chemical use, greenhouse gas emissions, and waste.

The Publishing and Knowledge Division follows the recommended standards for paper use set by the Green Press Initiative. The majority of our books are printed on Forest Stewardship Council (FSC)–certified paper, with nearly all containing 50–100 percent recycled content. The recycled fiber in our book paper is either unbleached or bleached using totally chlorine free (TCF), processed chlorine free (PCF), or enhanced elemental chlorine free (EECF) processes.

More information about the Bank's environmental philosophy can be found at http://crinfo.worldbank.org/wbcrinfo/node/4.